ANCIENT INDIAN EDUCATION

AN INQUIRY INTO ITS ORIGIN, DEVELOPMENT, AND IDEALS

BY

REV. F. E. KEAY, M.A.

VOLUME-III

COSMO PUBLICATIONS
NEW DELHI INDIA
1980

Made in India
This COSMO Edition 1992

Published by:
RANI KAPOOR (MRS.)
COSMO PUBLICATIONS
24-B, Ansari Road, Daryaganj,
New Delhi-110002.
India.

Printed in Mehra Offset Press.

PREFACE

THE history of the ancient education of India is to a large extent an unexplored tract. Except for a short sketch in Laurie's *Historical Survey of Pre-Christian Education*, and outlines of the subject in cyclopædias, or references scattered in various books, hardly anything has been written on the subject. With regard to Muhammadan Education in India, however, Mr. Narendra Nath Law's recently published book on the *Promotion of Learning by Muhammadans* has brought together some most useful evidence.

In attempting to write about the ancient education of India, one of the greatest difficulties has been to ascertain all the available material. The literature of India is very bulky, and only a small portion of it has been translated into English. References in it to education are not always numerous, and are scattered here and there amongst a vast amount of other material. I am well aware, therefore, that there may be more material available than I have yet been able to discover. The present attempt must be looked upon largely as a pioneer effort, but I hope that it may stimulate others also who are interested in Indian education to take up the work of research.

Throughout the long centuries of India's history educational development was taking place. It began away back in the times when the hymns of the Vedas were being composed, and has gone on until the present time. The first beginnings were in connection with the sacrificial ritual, and this system of Brāhmanic education has had a continuous history from that time till now. It is to this that our attention will first be given. The introduction of Buddhism and its growth into a widespread religion under the patronage and favour of powerful monarchs brought a new influence into Indian education; for although Buddhism was closely connected in its origin with the more ancient forms of religion, it was not under Brāhman control. The Muhammadan conquest brought a foreign influence into Indian social life, and the establishment of a form of education which had no connection with that of the Brāhmans. The education of the young nobles, corresponding to the knightly education of the Middle Ages of Europe, and the education of the craftsmen and of women also deserve our attention, as well as the system of popular education which grew up at some time in India and was in full swing when education came under the influence and control of the British Government.

In 1835 a momentous decision was made by the Government of Lord William Bentinck, acting on the advice of Macaulay's famous minute, to make English the medium of instruction in higher education in India. This largely accelerated the permeation of Indian life and ideas by Western thought, and has been one of the most powerful factors in producing that intellectual, social, political, and religious ferment which is going on in India to-day. Education in India has come under Western control and is being influenced by Western ideas. The spread of education in India is one of the most striking features of its present development, and already some of its most noble sons have believed that the time has come when it should be extended to all. Grave responsibilities rest upon those who have the control of Indian education to see that its development shall be on such lines as may be most suitable to the country, and likely to bring out the very best that is in the various races that inhabit the Indian Empire. Any attempt to foist even the most satisfactory of European systems of education upon India would be doomed to failure, and even if successful would be a great disaster. India may learn and is learning from the West many useful lessons in all subjects, and in educational thought and practice no less than in others; but if a system is to be evolved for India which shall be truly Indian, it must, while assimilating much that is Western, also gather up what is best and most useful from its own ancient systems and weave them into the complex whole that is being built up. For this reason the study of ancient Indian education is most important, and deserving of far more attention than it has hitherto received. And it may be that in the investigation certain points will be brought out that may not be without interest even for Western educators.

Amongst those who have given advice or suggestions I have specially to thank the Rev. Dr. H. U. Weitbrecht-Stanton, who read through the first draft of the chapter on Muhammadan Education, and made some valuable criticisms; and also Dr. J. N. Farquhar, to whom I am most deeply indebted for his interest and readiness to give counsel with regard to many points about which I have consulted him throughout. I am specially indebted to him for many suggestions with regard to the chapter on Brāhmanic education, and for reading the whole work in manuscript with great care, and suggesting many improvements.

[illegible] could be a great disaster [illegible] for India [illegible] to become [illegible] from the West [illegible] in [illegible] and in educational thought and practice [illegible] in other [illegible] for those who [illegible] not only [illegible] times, with [illegible] East and Western [illegible] up [illegible] and [illegible] us the [illegible] [illegible] them into the [illegible] is both [illegible]

[illegible] education than the [illegible] — but it may be that in a careful investigation certain points will be brought out that may not be without interest even to Western educationists.

Amongst those who have given advice or suggestions I have specially to thank the Rev. Dr. A. J. [illegible], Oxford, who read through the first draft of the chapter on Brahmanic Education and made some valuable criticisms; and also Dr. L. K. [illegible], to whom I am most deeply indebted for his interest and readiness to give counsel with regard to [illegible] about which I have consulted him. [illegible] I am especially indebted to him for many suggestions with regard to the Brahmanic Education, and for reading the whole work in manuscript with great care, and suggesting many improvements.

[illegible]

CONTENTS

CHAPTER I

BRĀHMANIC EDUCATION

WITHIN the boundaries of the modern Indian Empire there dwells a population of over three hundred millions, derived from different sources and speaking many different languages. Among the races four main types have been distinguished, namely, Dravidian, Aryan, Scythian, and Mongolian, and besides these, other races, in smaller numbers, have been introduced into India at different periods of the history, such as Parsees, Arabs, Turks, Afghans, Moguls, and, at a later date, some of the European races like the Portuguese and the English. The main types have not been kept distinct, but there has been a fusion of races on a large scale. The Dravidians represent the earliest known inhabitants of India; but it is the Aryan race that has had the greatest influence in controlling its destiny.

The Aryans entered India by the defiles of the north-west at some unknown date before 1000 B.C. There were probably several waves of invasion, and each tribe pushed its predecessor farther east or south. The influence of this race is not, however, to be judged by its numbers, or the extent of territory which was occupied. Not only did Aryan princes establish dynasties in many parts of India, but it was the Aryans, and especially the priestly class, the Brāhmans, who moulded the religion, philosophy, science, and art, as well as the social organization which is spread all over India. At the time when they entered the Panjāb they were divided into many tribes or clans governed by chieftains. The father had great power as head of the family. There were different classes amongst the Aryans, but these had not yet hardened into castes. These classes were the nobles or chieftains and their families, the priestly families, and the mass of the people who were chiefly employed in agriculture and cattle-rearing. The Dravidians were their common foes, but those captured in war became domestic slaves. The religion of the Aryans was a form of nature worship. The vault of heaven, the dawn, the winds, the lightning are considered the activities of personal gods to whom sacrifice and praise are offered. Worship is carried on in the open without temples or idols. Indra, Agni, and Soma are the deities to whom hymns are most often addressed.

Our knowledge of this period is derived from the *Saṁhitās* (collections of verses) of the *Vedas*, which form the oldest strata of Indian literature. The *Ṛigveda* was the earliest of these collections. It contains 1017 hymns divided into ten different books or *maṇḍalas*. The composition of these hymns took place at some time previous to 1000 B.C., while the Aryan race still occupied territories on both sides of the Indus.[1] Of the collection of ten books, it is considered by scholars that Books ii. to vii. formed the original nucleus.[2] Each of these seven is ascribed to a different seer (*ṛishi*), and was probably the work of himself and his descendants. They were thus family collections handed down from generation to generation, and no doubt guarded jealously as a family inheritance. It had become the custom for chieftains or nobles to appoint *purohitas*, or domestic priests, to bring them prosperity by sacrifice, and it was probably in such priestly families of high standing that the collections of hymns were formed and preserved, and the competition among these families to

[1] Macdonell, *Sans. Lit.*, p. 40.

[2] *Ibid.*, p. 43.

possess the best hymns led to the formation of a dignified and expressive literary dialect. As the influence of the priests increased, the ritual of the sacrifice became more complex. The technical lore of language and of hymns was handed down from father to son, and this was no doubt the beginning of Brāhmanic education. In a hymn [1] belonging to one of these early books there is a reference to what was probably the earliest form of the Brāhmanic school in India. It is a poem which compares the meeting together of the Brāhmans with the gathering of frogs in the rainy season :—

> 'Each of these twain receives the other kindly, while they are revelling in the flow of waters.
> When the frog moistened by the rain springs forward, and Green and Spotty both combine their voices.
> When one of these repeats the other's language, as he who learns the lesson of the teacher,
> Your every limb seems to be growing larger, as ye converse with eloquence on the waters.'

Each experienced priest probably taught his sons or nephews the ritual lore and hymns which were traditional in the family, by letting them repeat them over and over again after him until all had been committed to memory, and probably each family guarded the secrecy of its own sacred tradition.

At some time and in some way unknown these family collections came to be amalgamated and taught together. This may have been due to the action of some powerful chieftain who wished to gather for his own benefit all the sacrificial literature. The first and eighth books were then added at some time, and also the ninth, which consists of hymns used for the Soma sacrifice. The tenth book was added last of all, and although it contains some old material, some of it was written later. One hymn [2] in it refers to

[1] *Ṛigveda*, vii. 103, Griffith's trans.
[2] *Ibid.*, x. 90.

caste, and it is evident that by this time social distinctions had increased and society become more complex. In a hymn[1] of this last book there is reference to the learned Brāhmans meeting together for debate:—

'All friends are joyful in the friend who cometh in triumph, having conquered in assembly.
He is their blame averter, food provider; prepared is he and fit for deed of vigour.
One plies his constant task reciting verses; one sings the holy psalm in Sakvari measures.
One more, the Brāhman, tells the lore of being, and one lays down the rules of sacrificing.'

It is possible that the success in debate may refer to the passing of some test required before a young Brāhman was considered eligible to take part in the sacrificial ritual.[2]

The gathering together of all the hymns into one collection took place probably before 1000 B.C. When this was done it is likely that the schools where the priestly lore was learnt were no longer always family schools, though in many cases no doubt the boy was pupil to his own father. This indeed was often so in much later times.[3]

The word *Veda* really means 'knowledge', from the root *vid*, 'to know', and so was used to designate the sacred lore or collection of sacred literature. The *Ṛigveda* means the 'Veda of hymns', from *ṛich*, 'a laudatory stanza'. This collection of sacred poems was probably made not so much to preserve them as literature, but because they were needed for sacrificial use.

There were three functions which the priest might perform in the ritual, and to those who performed them different names were given. The *hotṛi* was the leading priest, and while the sacrifice was being made he recited poems or hymns of praise

[1] *Ṛigveaa*, x. 71.
[2] Compare the 'Responsio' of the Middle Ages in Europe.
[3] Cf. *e.g. Chhānd. Up.*, v. 3, 5; *Bṛih. Ār. Up.*, vi. 2, 4.

in honour of the particular god he was worshipping (Indra, Agni, etc.). Another part of the ritual was concerned with the *soma* sacrifice. *Soma* [1] was really a juice pressed out from a certain plant, which on account of its exhilarating and invigorating action came to be regarded as a divine drink which bestowed everlasting life. It was afterwards hypostatized and regarded as a god, and a special ritual grew up in connection with which hymns were sung. The priest who sang these *sāmans* was called an *udgātṛi*. Another priest was concerned with the manual acts of sacrificing, and he was called an *adhvaryu*. There was at first, however, no distinct order, and each priest might perform any of these functions. There was but one education for all, and each priestly student received a triple training so that he might perform any one of these three duties. Gradually, however, the ritual of the sacrifices became elaborated, and with its growing complexity some division of priestly labour became unavoidable. No one priest could become an expert in the three branches of ritual, and specialist training became necessary. Probably at first it consisted in a priestly student first learning the ritual of all three branches and then specializing in one of them. The collection of Soma hymns into the ninth book of the *Ṛigveda* seems to show traces of this. But eventually something more than this was needed, and there came to be three orders of priests, each possessing its own particular Veda, and having its own training schools. This probably took place at some time between 1000 and 800 B.C.

The *udgātṛi* had to learn to sing all the tunes required for the Soma ritual, and to know which particular strophe was required for each sacrifice. All the stanzas to be chanted at the Soma sacrifice were gathered into a separate collection called the *Sāmaveda*. All its verses except seventy-five were taken from the *Ṛigveda*, and form a special musical collection,

[1] Macdonell, *Sans. Lit.*, pp. 98 ff.

or sacrificial liturgy, for the Soma ritual.[1] It consists of two parts called *ārchikas*. The first *ārchika* consists of stanzas, each of which was associated with a separate tune, of which there were no less than 585. The second part, or *uttarārchika*, contains the strophes which were required for use in the ritual. The complicated work of the *udgātṛi* priest thus led to the creation of a special school for young Brāhmans who wished to specialize in this branch of study. At a later date, when writing began to be used, tune books called *gānas* were prepared.

Although the recitation of the appropriate hymns of praise at the ordinary sacrifices was the special duty of the *hotṛi* priest, the *adhvaryu*, who performed the manual acts of the sacrifice, was required to utter certain ritual formulas (*yajūṃshi*), and at different points of the ritual had also to utter certain prayers and praises. For the training of the *adhvaryu* priests also, special schools arose, and their particular Veda was the *Yajurveda*.[2] This collection consists of prose formulas or *mantras*, among which many verses, mostly taken from the *Ṛigveda*, are also interpolated. When these special schools were formed for the *udgātṛi* and *adhvaryu* priests, the older schools connected with the *Ṛigveda* came to be regarded as special schools for the *hotṛi* priests. Up to this time it would seem that only young Brāhmans were admitted to these schools, but there seems to have been no hard-and-fast distinction between the three orders of priests, and a priest might exercise any or all of the three functions if only he had received the necessary training. These three Vedas alone were originally recognized as canonical collections. But somewhat later there came to be recognized a fourth Veda known as the *Atharvaveda*.[3] It took a long time to establish its position, and even to this day in certain parts of South India it is almost unknown.

[1] Macdonell, *Sans. Lit.*, pp. 171 ff. [2] *Ibid.*, pp. 174 ff.
[3] *Ibid.*, pp. 185 ff.

It is a book of magic and sorcery, and consists of spells, which were used by the incantation priest. Most of these spells are to be used against hostile agencies such as diseases, animals, demons, wizards, and foes; but some are of an auspicious nature and intended to bring prosperity and good luck. In connection with this Veda another kind of specialist school arose.

By the time these various types of priestly schools had been formed the centre of the Aryan civilization had shifted eastwards and lay somewhere between the Sutlej and the Jumna rivers. There came to be slight differences in the Vedic texts, and each recension was called a *śākhā*. Those who followed a particular *śākhā* of a Veda were said to form a *charana*, or school, of that Veda. At some time, however, precautions were taken for the preservation of the sacred text, and this led to the constitution of the *padapāṭha*[1] and other forms of the sacred texts.

The different kinds of priestly schools had now become well developed, and were learned associations with a growing reputation, and a priest was proud of the school in which he had received his training, and he could not perform his duties as priest without having passed through one of these schools. The first duty of the student was to learn by heart the particular Veda of his school. This he did by repeating it after his teacher until perfect accuracy was secured. The method was entirely oral, and it was not till much later times that writing was introduced. He would also receive a great deal of instruction on his duties as a priest of the particular school in which he was studying, and also explanations of the meaning of the hymns and ritual acts. The instruction was called *vidhi*, the explanation *arthavāda*. For a long time these lectures were given by the teacher as he willed in his own language, but in each school this didactic material tended to become more and

[1] See below, pp. 38 f., and Macdonell, *Sans. Lit.*, p. 51.

more in accordance with precedent, and finally became stereotyped in the *Brāhmaṇas*.[1] These works are in prose, and were composed somewhere between 800 and 500 B.C. The *Brāhmaṇas* are connected with the different Vedic schools, and contain such material as the students of each Veda required, but their general characteristics are the same. Besides instruction and explanation relating to the sacrificial ritual, they contain mythological stories and legends, speculation, and argument, and we can find in them the first beginnings of grammar, astronomy, etymology, philosophy, and law. Their intellectual activity was centred, however, on the sacrifice, and much of the matter contained in them seems meaningless and puerile to the modern mind. They exhibit an arrogant sacerdotalism, but at the same time signs of considerable intellectual vigour. The language of the old hymns had now become archaic, and unintelligible to the multitude. This is referred to in the *Śatapatha Brāhmaṇa*,[2] and was no doubt one of the reasons why the power of the priesthood increased.

The Aryans had now advanced further into India, and it is perhaps to this period that we are to ascribe the events which form the historical basis of the two great epics, the *Mahābhārata* and the *Rāmāyaṇa*. During this period there was a growth of luxury. The power of the king has become greater, and he employs an army of hired soldiers. The supremacy of the priesthood is being established, and the priest is coming to be regarded no longer as a servant or companion of the king, but as his superior. The classes were becoming hardened into caste divisions, and besides the Brāhmans (priests), Kshatriyas (nobles and warriors), and Vaiśyas (agriculturists and traders), who were of Aryan descent, though probably by this time mixed with non-Aryans, the great mass of non-Aryan peoples were classed as Śūdras. In course

[1] Macdonell, *Sans. Lit.*, p. 202.
[2] *Śatap. Br.*, iii. 2, 1, 24.

of time these castes became divided into many more, and every social distinction created by occupation, or race, or language tended to produce a separate caste.

In the *Atharvaveda*[1] there is a mystic hymn which describes the sun, or the primeval principle, under the figure of a Brāhman student (*brahmachārī*), who brings firewood and alms for his teacher. This offering of firewood to a teacher became the regular way by which a youth sought to be recognized as his pupil, and implied a desire to partake in his domestic sacrifice and to accept the duty of helping to maintain it. It also came to be a duty for students to collect alms for their own support and that of their teacher. From the *Brāhmaṇas* we can get some idea of the early development of the educational system of the Brāhmans. In the *Śatapatha Brāhmaṇa*, for instance, we are given a line of succession of teachers who have transmitted the sacrificial science.[2] This line is traced back to Prajāpati, and Brāhman students are spoken of as guarding their teacher, his house and cattle, lest he should be taken from them.[3] There are references also to a lad going to a teacher with firewood in his hand and asking to become his pupil,[4] and to students collecting alms and fuel for their teacher.[5] This *Brāhmaṇa* also contains an account of the Upanayana, or initiation, of the Brāhmanical student.[6] 'He says, "I have come for *brahmacharya*" (studentship); he thereby reports himself to the Brāhman. He says, "Let me be a *brahmachārī*" (student); he thereby makes himself over to the Brāhman. He (the teacher) then says, "What is thy name?" . . . He then takes his (right) hand with, "Indra's disciple thou art; Agni is thy teacher; I am thy teacher, O N. N.!" He then commits him to the beings: "To Prajāpati I commit

[1] *Atharvaveda*, xi. 5.

[2] *Śatap. Br.*, x. 6, 5, 9.

[3] *Ibid.*, iii. 2, 6, 15.

[4] *Ibid.*, xi. 4, 1, 9.

[5] *Ibid.*, xi. 3, 3.

[6] *Ibid.*, xi. 5, 4.

thee ; to the god Savitṛi I commit thee. . . . To the waters, to the plants I commit thee. . . . To Heaven and Earth I commit thee. . . . To all beings I commit thee for security from injury. Thou art a *brahmachārī* . . . sip water . . . do thy work . . . put on fuel . . . do not sleep . . . sip water."' 'Sip water' is explained as meaning 'sip ambrosia'. 'He thus encloses him on both sides with ambrosia.' "He then recites to him (teaches him) the *sāvitrī*.'

It was already becoming recognized that for the study of the Vedic learning a long period of studentship was necessary. In the *Taittirīya Brāhmaṇa* we read[1]—

'Bharadvāja lived through three lives in the state of a religious student. Indra approached him when he was lying old and decrepit, and said to him, "Bharadvāja, if I give thee a fourth life, how wilt thou employ it?" "I will lead the life of a religious student," he replied. He (Indra) showed him three mountain-like objects, as it were unknown. From each of them he took a handful, and, calling to him, "Bharadvāja", said, "These are the three Vedas. The Vedas are infinite. This is what thou hast studied during these three lives. Now there is another thing which thou hast not studied; come and learn it. This is the universal science. . . . He who knows this (*ya evam veda*) conquers a world as great as he would gain by the triple Vedic science."'

We have already seen how the influence of the priesthood had been growing and the ritual of the sacrifice enormously developed. But there must always have been some earnest seekers after truth who were not satisfied with sacrificial ritual. Already in some of the latest hymns of the *Ṛigveda* there are traces of philosophical speculation. Men were asking what the universe is and how it came into being, what the soul of man is, and what law governs birth and death. These and other great questions were troubling the minds of thoughtful

[1] *Taitt. Br.*, iii. 10, 11, 3.

persons, and those who sought an answer to them often forsook home and family and worldly duties and retired to the forests, where they spent their time in asceticism and meditation. This religious ferment was contributed to not only by Brāhmans, but by many religious laymen. At the end of the *Brāhmaṇas* are certain treatises known as *Āraṇyakas*,[1] or 'forest-books'. They are allegorical expositions of the sacrificial ritual, and are considered to be the *Brāhmaṇas* of the *Vānaprasthas*, an order of forest hermits that appeared about this time, who no longer performed the actual sacrifices, but only meditated on them. Some, however, have considered them to be treatises which, on account of their mystic sanctity, were only to be communicated in the solitude of the forest. They form a transition to the *Upanishads*, which are often embedded in them. These are treatises wholly given up to philosophical speculation, and represent the last stage of the Brāhmaṇa literature. The higher philosophical knowledge which they set forth came to be recognized as the *Vedānta* (end of the Veda)—the completion and crown of Vedic learning. These treatises were composed some time between 800 and 500 B.C. The leading ideas of this philosophical speculation are that the world has been evolved from the *Ātman*, or Universal Soul, and that this is also the Self within us. The inequalities of human life are explained by the doctrines of *karma* and transmigration.

From the *Upanishads* we get many more sidelights on the ancient Brāhmanic education. The meaning of the word 'Upanishad' has been the matter of discussion. Max Müller[2] says that 'Upanishad,' besides being the recognized title of certain philosophical treatises, occurs also in the sense of doctrine and of secret doctrine, and that it seems to have assumed this meaning from having been used originally in the

[1] Macdonell, *Sans. Lit.*, p. 204.
[2] *S.B.E.*, vol. i. p. lxxx.

sense of session or assembly, in which one or more pupils receive instruction from a teacher. These treatises profess to give a kind of esoteric doctrine, or higher enlightenment, and refer to pupils as having studied all the Vedas and sacrificial ritual, and yet without the knowledge of the answers to the deeper philosophical speculations which troubled earnest seekers after truth. Śvetaketu Aruṇeya was a Brāhman youth who was sent to school by his father. 'Having [1] begun his apprenticeship (with a teacher) when he was twelve years of age, Śvetaketu returned to his father when he was twenty-four, having then studied all the Vedas—conceited, considering himself well-read, and stern.

'His father said to him: "Śvetaketu, as you are so conceited, considering yourself well-read, and so stern, my dear, have you ever asked for that instruction by which we hear what cannot be perceived, by which we know what cannot be known?"'

Śvetaketu having expressed his ignorance of this deep teaching, his father proceeds to instruct him.

It would seem that at this period it was not the universal custom for a Brāhman youth to enter upon a life of studentship. Thus Śvetaketu's father said to him,[2] 'Śvetaketu, go to school, for there is none belonging to our race, darling, who, not having studied (the Veda), is, as it were, a Brāhman by birth only'. So also the entrance [3] of Satyakāma, son of Jabālā, upon studentship seems to be his own voluntary choice. It was still often the custom for a son to receive instruction at the hands of his father, as in the case of Śvetaketu,[4] but he often went to other teachers.[5] When a student wished to

[1] *Chhānd. Up.*, vi. 1, 2, 3.

[2] *Ibid.*, vi. 1, 1. For education as reflected in the *Upanishads*, see art. on *āsrama* by Deussen in *E.R.E.*

[3] *Chhānd. Up.*, iv. 4, 1.

[4] *Ibid.*, v. 3, 1; *Bṛih. Ār. Up.*, vi. 2, 1; *Kaush. Up.*, i. 1.

[5] *Chhānd. Up.*, vi. 1, 1.

become a pupil of any teacher, the recognized way of making application to him was to approach him with fuel in the hands as a sign that the pupil wished to serve him and help to maintain his sacred fire. 'Let[1] him, in order to understand this, take fuel in his hand and approach a *guru* who is learned and dwells entirely in *Brahman*.' It seems to have been usual for the teacher to make an inquiry into the birth and family of the applicant before receiving him as a pupil, as in the case of Satyakāma.[2] In this case the inquiry was made in a very indulgent manner, but it seems to show that it was still the rule only for Brāhmans to be received as students. One instance is given where instruction was granted without any formal reception.[3]

As in the *Brāhmaṇas*, the necessity for a long period of studentship is recognized. Thus Indra is said to have lived with Prajāpati as a pupil no less than one hundred and five years.[4] The actual duration of studentship was coming to be recognized as twelve years.[5] During this period of twelve years we are told that Śvetaketu studied all the Vedas, which differs from the later regulation of twelve years for each Veda. In the case of Śvetaketu, however, it may have been only the hymns of the three Vedas that he learned, as this is what his father expected from him.[6] In the same *Upanishad*, however, we have what seems to be an exhaustive list of all that was studied in those days, and which includes a good deal more than a knowledge of the hymns of the three Vedas.[7]

'Nārada approached Sanatkumāra and said, "Teach me, Sir!" Sanatkumāra said to him: "Please to tell me what you know; afterwards I shall tell you what is beyond."

'Nārada said: "I know the Ṛigveda, Sir, the Yajurveda,

[1] *Muṇḍ. Up.*, I, 2, 12. There are several other references in the *Upanishads*.

[2] *Chhānd. Up.*, iv. 4, 4.

[3] *Ibid.*, v. 11, 7.

[4] *Ibid.*, viii. ii. 3.

[5] *Ibid.*, iv. 10, 1; vi. 1, 2.

[6] *Ibid.*, vi. 7, 2.

[7] *Ibid.*, vii. 1, 1, 2.

the Sāmaveda, as the fourth the Ārtharvana, as the fifth the Itihāsa-purāṇa (the Bhārata); the Veda of the Vedas (grammar); the Pitrya (the rules for the sacrifices for the ancestors); the Rāśi (the science of numbers); the Daiva (the science of portents); the Nidhi (the science of time); the Vākovākya (logic); the Ekāyana (ethics); the Devavidyā (etymology); the Brahmavidyā (pronunciation, *śikshā*, ceremonial, *kalpa*, prosody, *chhandas*); the Bhūtavidyā (the science of demons); the Kshatravidyā (the science of weapons); the Nakshatravidyā (astronomy); the Sarpa- and Devajanavidyā (the science of serpents or poisons, and the sciences of the genii, such as the making of perfumes, dancing, singing, playing, and other fine arts). All this I know, Sir. . . .''

The *Bṛihadāraṇyaka Upanishad* gives a somewhat similar list,[1] namely, 'Ṛigveda, Yajurveda, Sāmaveda, Atharvāngirasas,[2] Itihāsa (legends), Purāna (cosmogonies), Vidyā (knowledge), the Upanishads, Ślokas (verses), Sūtras (prose rules), Anuvyākhyānas (glosses), Vyākhyānas (commentaries)

These extracts show how the curriculum of the Brāhmanic schools was developing.

The period of studentship was, however, looked upon not only as a time of learning, but as a time of vigorous discipline. There are some instances in the *Upanishads* where no teaching was given for several years after studentship had begun,[3] but these seem to be exceptional cases. Pupils had to work for their teacher in house and field, attending to his sacred fires,[4] looking after his cattle,[5] and collecting alms for him.[6] The pupil also accompanied his teacher and awaited his

[1] *Bṛih. Ār. Up.*, ii. 4, 10.

[2] *I.e.* the *Atharvaveda.*

[3] Upakosala in *Chhānd. Up.*, iv. 10, 1, 2; Satyakāma in *Chhānd. Up.*, iv. 4, 5.

[4] *Chhānd. Up.*, iv. 10, 1.

[5] *Ibid.*, iv. 4, 5.

[6] *Ibid.*, iv. 3, 5.

commands.[1] 'In the leisure time left from the duties to be performed for the *guru*'[2] the Veda was studied.

It seems to have been the custom in those days for students sometimes to travel far and wide[3] in order to attach themselves to celebrated teachers. Renowned teachers also itinerated from place to place,[4] and there were those to whom pupils came from all sides 'as waters run downwards, as the months go to the year'.[5] As a rule, however, a student remained in the house of his teacher till the conclusion of his studies, when he entered upon married life. On his dismissal the pupil received admonition from his teacher. 'After[6] having taught the Veda, the teacher instructs the pupil: "Say what is true! Do thy duty! Do not neglect the study of the Veda! After having brought to thy teacher his proper reward, do not cut off the line of children! Do not swerve from the truth! Do not swerve from duty! Do not neglect what is useful! Do not neglect greatness! Do not neglect the learning and teaching of the Veda!"' etc.

In some cases, however, the student might choose to become a life-long pupil of his teacher,[7] and in others to retire to the woods as a forest hermit, or *vānaprastha*.[8]

The *Upanishads* show us the theory of the four *āśramas*, or stages of life, in process of formation. The word *āśrama* (from the root *śram*, to exert oneself, or to perform austerities) means first of all a place where austerities are performed, or a hermitage, and secondly, the action of performing austerities. So the period of studentship of the *brahmachārī* was regarded as a time of discipline, or an *āśrama*. But the Brāhmanical system tended to extend the idea of *āśrama* over the whole life. Thus after the period of studentship a young man might

[1] *Bṛih. Ār. Up.*, iii. 1, 2.
[2] *Chhānd. Up.*, viii. 15, 1.
[3] *Bṛih. Ār. Up.*, iii. 3, 1; iii. 7. 1.
[4] *Kaush. Up.*, iv. 1.
[5] *Taitt. Up.*, 1, 4, 3.
[6] *Ibid.*, 1, 11.
[7] *Bṛih. Ār. Up.*, ii. 23, 2.
[8] *Chhānd. Up.*, ii. 23, 1.

enter upon the second stage, that of a *gṛihastha*, or householder. Then after having brought up a family and done his duty in the world he could enter upon the life of a *vānaprastha*, or forest hermit, and later became a *sannyāsī*, or wandering ascetic, who had separated himself from all attachment to the world, and having attained the knowledge of the *Ātman*, waited only for death to bring about his final emancipation. But this complete theory of four *āśramas* was not worked out all at once. In the *Upanishads* we see only its beginnings. Thus in one passage in the *Chhāndogya Upanishad* there is mention of only the student and the householder, while in another[2] passage the asceticism (*tapas*) of the hermit is mentioned along with these as a third branch of duty. They are not, however, regarded so much as a progressive series as alternatives.[3] These passages also refer only to three *āśramas*, and contrast with them the man who knows the *Ātman*. The position of the latter came in course of time to be regarded as a fourth *āśrama*. It was not, however, till much later times that the third and fourth were clearly separated, and the complete theory of the four stages worked out. When this was done the whole of life was looked upon as an education for the life beyond with four distinct stages, of which the life of studentship was only the first, though we cannot tell to what extent the practice corresponded to the theory, and it would seem likely that the ideal was never fully attained except by the few.

In the early Vedic schools it seems that instruction was confined to young Brāhmans, and was regarded mainly as a preparation for their future vocation as priests, but at some time before 500 B.C. the education of the young Kshatriyas and Vaiśyas had also come under Brāhman control, and in

[1] *Chhānd. Up.*, viii. 15, 1.
[2] *Ibid.*, ii. 23, 2.
[3] See also passages in *Bṛih. Ār. Up.*, iv. 4, 22; iii. 5, 1; iii. 8, 10.

their case was an opportunity of inculcating in their minds the necessary directions for all their future life. It became also the exclusive privilege of the Brāhmans to give this instruction, and this marks the growing influence of the priesthood. The ceremony of initiation and investiture with the sacred thread came to be regarded for all the Aryan youth as the preliminary to school life. The three castes which had this privilege, namely, the Brāhmans, Kshatriyas, and Vaiśyas, were called *dvija*, or 'twice-born', because the ceremony of initiation was looked upon as a second birth.

By the time, then, that the various portions of the Veda had been completed, Brāhmanic education was not only of long standing, but was highly organized, and the literature of the next period shows elaborate rules formed for its regulation. This literature is known as the *Sūtras*, and came into being from about 600 to 200 B.C. The sacred books which had to be mastered by the student had increased to a huge bulk, and it was necessary to condense their teaching into some convenient form. *Sūtras*, or 'threads', consist of aphorisms, or pithy phrases, in which condensation and brevity have been carried out to such an extent that the result is often an obscurity which can only be explained by a commentary. There was a saying that the saving of one syllable in a Sūtra gave more pleasure than the birth of a son, the force of which can only be understood when we remember how important it was considered that every Hindu should have a son to succeed him and perform the sacrificial rites after his death. The rules which applied to education are contained in the *Dharma*[1] *Sūtras*. *Dharma* is 'one[2] of the most comprehensive and important terms in the whole of Sanskrit literature'. It includes the ideas of sacred law and duty, justice, religious merit, religion, and morality. It is applied to

[1] Also in the *Grihya Sūtras*.

[2] See *E.R.E.*, vol. iv., p. 702, article on 'Dharma', by J. Jolly.

the established practice or custom of any caste or community. That which a man is expected to do because of his position in life or his caste is his *dharma*. During the early centuries of Brāhmanic education the *dharma* relating to education as well as to other matters had been gradually formed, and we have already seen something of this process going on. The composition of the Sūtras helped to fix the *dharma* and so to stereotype a great deal of the social system, including the educational theory and practice of the schools. The oldest existing *Dharma Sūtras* are considered by scholars to be those of Gautama, and their date is supposed to be about 500 B.C.[1] The *Dharma Sūtras* contain regulations relating to social life, and amongst other things have many rules dealing with the duties of teachers and students. It must be remembered, of course, that these rules, though composed about 500 B.C., give an account of practice which must have been still more ancient. There are other extant *Dharma Sūtras*, besides those of Gautama, *e.g.* those of Āpastamba, Vasishtha, and Baudhāyana, which probably come a little later, and the great Law Book of India, the Code of Manu, is a metrical work, supposed by scholars to date from about 200 A.D., but to be based upon a much older *Mānava Dharma Sūtra*,[2] which is no longer extant.

There were many sacred rites or sacraments (*saṃskāras*) to be performed from the time of conception onwards. The *upanayana*, or initiation ceremony, was that sacrament by which a lad of the three 'twice-born' castes entered upon studentship. Gautama says,[3] 'The initiation of a Brāhman shall ordinarily take place in his eighth year. (It may also be performed) in the ninth or fifth (years) for the fulfilment of (some particular) wish. The number of years (is to be calculated) from conception. That (initiation) is the second

[1] Macdonell, *Sans. Lit.*, p. 260.
[2] *Ibid.*, p. 428.
[3] Gautama, i. 5–14.

birth. . . . The initiation of a Kshatriya (shall ordinarily take place) in the eleventh (year after conception), and that of a Vaiśya in the twelfth. Up to the sixteenth year the time for the *sāvitrī* (initiation) of a Brāhman has not passed. Nor (for the initation) of a Kshatriya up to the twentieth (year). (And the limit for that) of a Vaiśya (extends) two years beyond (the latter term).' The other Sūtras contain similar regulations. The age fixed was no doubt regarded as the ideal to be aimed at, though we see that considerable latitude was provided for. A young Brāhman was thus about seven years of age (according to our reckoning) when he entered upon the obligations of studentship, and this age is that which has been considered a suitable one by many educationists. It was expressly provided in a later verse that a child should not be made to recite Vedic verses before initiation;[1] but whether this excluded all study cannot be said. Why a later age was provided for Kshatriyas and Vaiśyas to commence their studies is not quite clear. They were, of course, not expected to attain to the same proficiency in the Vedic sciences as the young Brāhman, as he alone could perform the sacrificial ritual, and certain portions of the sacred knowledge were reserved for him, and their course was therefore, it may be supposed, not expected to last as long as his. But in this case we should have expected them to have started at the same time and to have left their studentship at an earlier age, especially as they had also to learn their own particular crafts. It seems probable, however, that the difference in age was to emphasize the supposed intellectual superiority of the Brāhman, who was thus ready to begin the study at a younger age than his non-Brāhman fellows.

There were regulations for the clothing of those who had become students.[2] The girdle or sacred cord worn after initiation varied in material according to the caste. For the

[1] Gautama, ii. 5.

[2] *Ibid.*, i. 15–27.

Brāhman it was to be of munja grass; for the Kshatriya, a bow-string; and for the Vaiśya, a woollen or hempen thread. The upper garments were to be skins of animals, again varying according to caste, and respectively, the skin of a black buck, a spotted deer, or a he-goat. For lower garments hemp, flax, or wool, or the inner bark of a certain tree were prescribed. Gautama says that these under-garments might also be of undyed cotton cloth, but if dyed the garment of a Brāhman should be dyed with red dye from a tree, and those of the other two castes with madder and turmeric respectively. The staves carried also varied according to caste, reaching, in the case of the Brāhman, to the crown of the head; in the case of the Kshatriya, to the forehead; and in the case of the Vaiśya, to the tip of the nose. The hair might be shaved or worn braided on the top, or there might be merely one lock left on the crown. The arrangement of hair was probably regulated by the custom of the family, school, or country.

Having accepted the position of student by the rite of initiation, to which we have already referred, the pupil was received into the household of his teacher. Sometimes, of course, the teacher might be his own father. But although he was thus made, as it were, a member of his teacher's family, and the teacher was bidden to love him as his own son, the pupil was subjected to a rigid discipline during his course of study. The length of the course varied according to the number of Vedas studied. 'He shall remain a student for twelve years in order to study one Veda. Or if he studies all the Vedas, twelve years for each. Or during as long a period as he requires for learning them.'[1] Thus, if all four Vedas were studied, the length of the course might be forty-eight years! Some of the authorities only recognize three Vedas (excluding the *Atharvaveda*), but even thirty-six years seems a long enough course even for the most enthusiastic. A great

[1] Gautama, ii. 45-47.

part of the work consisted of the committal to memory of the sacred texts and other writings, and the enormous bulk of these must have necessitated a long period of study. It seems hardly possible to believe that more than a few students continued their studies as long as even thirty-six years. Probably most were satisfied with the twelve years required for studying one Veda, and the twelve years prescribed for each of the Vedas may have been intended to emphasize their importance. Megasthenes, the Greek who visited India about 300 B.C., refers, however, to the Indian student spending thirty-seven years in study. The length of the annual term to be spent in Veda study was four and a half or five and a half months each year, and began usually at the full moon of the month *Śrāvaṇa* (July–Aug.)[1] It thus came during the rainy and cold seasons when the heat is less intense. Numerous holidays were also allowed, such as the new-moon and full-moon, days of certain months and other days which were set apart for various religious ceremonies. The authorities have also a long list of restrictions,[2] which prohibit the reading of the Veda when certain occurrences take place, as, for instance, when the wind whirls up dust in the daytime, or when the wind is audible at night, when the sound of a drum or of a chariot or of a person in pain is heard, when there is the barking of dogs and jackals, or the chattering of monkeys, when the sky was a brilliant red, or there was a rainbow, etc., etc. Some of these restrictions were no doubt dictated by superstition, others because the various sounds or phenomena betokened impending danger or discomfort, or because their distraction was not conducive to study. But all these possible hindrances must have reduced the actual time spent in learning.

The pupil was under certain obligations towards the teacher. In the first place, he was to remain with the teacher so long as his course lasted, and not to dwell with anybody

[1] Gautama, xvi. i, 2

[2] *Ibid.*, xvi.

else.[1] From the *Upanishads* one gets the impression that students sometimes wandered from teacher to teacher, but if that were so it must either have been irregular, or else was found to be attended with abuses, and afterwards restricted.

Certain menial services had to be performed by the pupil for his teacher. This included the fetching of water and collecting fuel, and sweeping the place round the fire. Begging for his food was also a duty which the student had to perform.[2] Food might be accepted from men of all castes except 'Abhiśastas and outcastes'[3] It was to be demanded if possible from strangers, but if no alms were to be obtained in that way the student might beg in the houses of his relations or even of his teacher.[4] When he returned from his begging tour the student had to announce to his teacher what he had received, and after receiving his permission he might eat according to the prescribed rules, 'in silence, contented, and without greed'.[5] In the Middle Ages in Europe we read of some students in the universities subsisting by means of begging; but India far surpassed that by making it a rule for all students, and even under modern conditions it is not at all uncommon for students to find their support in this way.

Rigid rules were laid down for the conduct of pupils. These included hygienic, moral, and religious precepts and the regulation of good manners. It was his duty to bathe daily, and to avoid[6] 'honey, meat, perfumes, garlands, sleep in the daytime, ointments, collyrium, a carriage, shoes, a parasol, love, anger, coveteousness, perplexity, garrulity, playing musical instruments, bathing (for mere pleasure), cleaning the teeth, elation, dancing, singing, calumny, and terror', and

[1] Gautama, iii. 5.
[2] Āpastamba, i. i.
[3] Gautama, ii. 35.
[4] *Ibid.*, ii 37.
[5] *Ibid.*, ii. 39-41.
[6] *Ibid.*, ii. 13; Manu, ii. 177, 178.

all pungent foods. In the presence of his teacher he must not cover his throat, cross his legs, or lean against a wall, or stretch out his feet.[1] 'Tongue, arms, and stomach' were to be kept in subjection.[2] Spitting, laughing, yawning, and cracking the joints of the fingers were also forbidden.[3] He was enjoined always to speak the truth, and to avoid bitter speeches.[4] He was always to speak in a respectful manner of superiors.[5] Gambling, 'low service' (perhaps menial service other than that prescribed), taking things not offered, and injuring animate beings were also unlawful for a student.[6] All Brāhmans were forbidden to use spirituous liquors.[7] Chastity was strictly enjoined, and the student was not even to gaze at or touch women.[8] In the morning and evening the pupil was bidden to perform his devotions outside the village. 'Silent he shall stand during the former, and sit during the latter, from (the time when one) light (is still visible) until (the other) light (appears).'[9] Oblations were also to be offered morning and evening to the sacred fire.[10]

There were rules also for the respect due from pupil to teacher. Strict obedience was enjoined unless the teacher ordered the pupil to commit crimes which involved loss of caste.[11] The pupil was on no account to contradict the teacher, and was always to occupy a seat or couch lower than the teacher.[12] He was always to rise in the morning before his teacher was up, and retire to rest at night after him.[13] If spoken to by the teacher he must, if lying or sitting, rise from his couch or seat before he answered, and when called by the teacher was to approach him even though he could not see

1 Gautama, ii. 14.
2 *Ibid.*, ii. 22.
3 *Ibid.*, ii. 15.
4 *Ibid.*, ii. 19; Manu, ii. 179.
5 Gautama, ii. 24.
6 *Ibid.*, ii. 17.
7 *Ibid.*, ii. 20.
8 *Ibid.*, ii. 16.
9 *Ibid.*, ii. 11.
10 *Ibid.*, ii. 8.
11 Āpastamba, i. 1.
12 *Ibid.*
13 Gautama, ii. 21.

him. If he saw the teacher standing or sitting in a lower place, or to the leeward or to the windward, he was to rise and change his position.[1] If the teacher walked, the student was to walk after him.[2] The teacher's name was not to be pronounced by the pupil, but if it was necessary to indicate it the pupil must do so by using a synonymous term.[3] Every morning the feet of the teacher were to be embraced by the pupil.[4] There were also rules enjoining respect for the sons and wives and other relatives of the teacher. In Manu these rules are even further elaborated.[5]

The teacher was also under obligation to fulfil his duty towards the pupil. Not only was he to love him as his own son, but he was to give him full attention in the teaching of the sacred science, and withhold no part of it from him.[6] He was not to use the pupil for his own purposes except in times of distress. After the rite of initiation has been performed his first duty was to instruct the pupil in the rules of personal purification, of conduct, of the fire worship, and of the twilight devotions. There is a passage in Manu[7] referring to the behaviour of the teacher towards his pupil which contains some excellent advice. It runs as follows :—

'Created beings must be instructed in what concerns their welfare without giving them pain, and sweet and gentle speech must be used by a teacher who desires to abide by the sacred law. He, forsooth, whose speech and thoughts are pure and ever perfectly guarded, gains the whole reward which is conferred by the Vedānta. Let him not, even though in pain, speak words cutting others to the quick; let him not injure others in thought or deed; let him not utter speeches which make others afraid of him, since that will prevent him from gaining heaven.'

[1] Gautama, ii. 25–27. [2] *Ibid.*, ii. 28. [3] *Ibid.*, ii. 18, 23.
[4] *Ibid.*, i. 52. [5] See Manu, ch. ii.
[6] Āpastamba, i. 2. [7] Manu, ii. 159–161.

These old-time teachers seem to have been against harsh punishments. Gautama says,[1] 'As a rule the pupil shall not be punished corporally. If no other course is possible he may be corrected with a thin rope or cane. If the teacher strikes him with any other instrument he shall be punished by the king'. Manu also allows [2] that a pupil who has committed faults 'may be beaten with a rope or split bamboo, but on the back part of the body only, never on a noble part; he who strikes them otherwise will incur the same guilt as a thief'. Āpastamba, however, allows [3] as punishments, 'frightening, fasting, bathing in cold water, and banishment from the teacher's presence'.

It was considered a duty for Brāhmans to teach, and all the time the pupil was under instruction the teacher was forbidden to accept a fee. When, however, the course was ended, it was the duty of the pupil to offer a present to his preceptor. Except possibly in the case of rich pupils it could never have been in any sense an adequate remuneration for services performed. Manu says,[4] 'He who knows the sacred law must not present any gift to his teacher before the *samāvartana* (rite performed by student on returning home); but when, with the permission of his teacher, he is about to take the (final) bath, let him procure a present for the venerable man according to his ability, viz. a field, a cow, a horse, a parasol and shoes, a seat, grain, even vegetables, and thus give pleasure to his teacher'.

After the course was completed the pupil performed certain bathing ceremonies, and was called a *snātaka*, that is, one who has bathed, and he was now ready to enter upon another of the four *āśramas*. In most cases he would marry and become a *grihastha*, but some passed at once to the state of a *vānaprastha* or *sannyāsī*.

[1] Gautama, ii. 42–44.
[2] Manu, viii. 299, 300.
[3] Āpastamba, i. 2.
[4] Manu, ii. 245, 246.

The foregoing account shows us an interesting and pleasing picture of the life of pupil and teacher in India dating back to many centuries before Christ. The pupil was under a somewhat rigorous discipline, but there was nothing harsh or brutal about it, and a high ideal of moral life and character was held before both pupil and teacher. The latter had no mercenary motive to impel him to teach, but was to perform his office solely as a duty which he owed towards others and his pupil in particular; and the pupil, on the other hand, was trained to a simple life, whether he was rich or poor, and habits of discipline, reverence, and self-respect were inculcated.

Coming now to the actual teaching Gautama tells us as follows [1] :—

'Taking hold with his right hand of the left hand of his teacher, but leaving the thumb free, the pupil shall address his teacher, saying, "Venerable Sir, recite!" He shall fix his eyes and his mind on the teacher. He shall touch with *kuśa* grass the seat of the vital airs (*i.e.* the organs of sense located in his head). He shall thrice restrain his breath for the space of fifteen moments. And he shall seat himself on blades of *kuśa* grass the tops of which are turned to the east. The five *vyāhṛitis* (*i.e.* the mystic words *Bhūḥ*, *Bhuvaḥ*, *Svaḥ*, *Satyam*, and *Purushaḥ*) must each be preceded by the syllable *Ōm* and with *Satya*. Every morning the feet of the teacher must be embraced by the pupil. And both at the beginning and at the end of a lesson in the Veda. After having received permission, the pupil shall sit down to the right of his teacher, turning his face towards the east or towards the north, and the *sāvitrī* must be recited. All these acts must be performed at the beginning of the instruction in the Veda. The syllable *Ōm* must precede the recitation of other parts of the Veda also.'

[1] Gautama, i. 46 ff.

Meaningless and trivial as many of these regulations seem to us, they were no doubt regarded as of great value by those who used them in those far-off days. They must have been intended to emphasize the great solemnity of the work in which pupil and teacher were engaged, and to impress upon the pupil the mysterious sacredness which was supposed to characterize the knowledge which was being passed on to him by his teacher. The first and foremost object which the teacher had before him was to hand down to the pupil the exact contents of the sacred books as he himself had received them, as well as of those sacrificial and other rules which it was necessary for the young Brāhman to know in order to perform his priestly functions.

The different Vedas arose, as we have seen, as collections primarily intended for different classes of priests. Every Brāhmanic family became devoted to the study of a particular Veda, and to a particular *śākhā* or recension of that Veda. The domestic rites of that family are performed according to the ritual described in the *Sūtras* connected with that Veda. It became then of the first importance that the exact text of that particular Veda, with the *Brāhmaṇas* and *Āraṇyakas* or *Upanishads*, as well as of the *Sūtras* attached to them, should be handed down from generation to generation. Now, writing was not known in India till 800 B.C., when it was introduced by traders coming by way of Mesopotamia. And although the complete Sanskrit alphabet on phonetic principles must have existed by 500 B.C., this being the alphabet recognized by the great grammarian, Pāṇini, who flourished in the fourth century B.C., writing was at first used chiefly for trading and other similar purposes, and it was a long time before it came to be used for the sacred books.[1] Probably these were considered too holy to be committed to writing, and there was

[1] For writing in India, see 'Buddhist India', T. W. Rhys Davids, pp. 107 ff.

also the fear that they might get into the hands of unauthorized persons. In course of time they were all committed to writing, but oral tradition was still the method relied on for handing down the sacred text. Max Müller states[1] that even nowadays, when there are not only manuscripts but also a printed text, the Vedas are still passed on in the Brāhmanic families by oral tradition. When one considers the enormous bulk of the sacred literature it would seem an almost impossible task for it to have been preserved all through so many centuries in this way. Still we know it was done and is being done down to the present time. We need not be surprised at the long period of twelve years which was considered necessary to become acquainted with even one Veda. Max Müller quotes[2] from a letter which he received in 1878 from an Indian gentleman giving an account of the system as it was then. 'A student of a *Ṛigveda Śākhā*, if sharp and assiduous, takes about eight years to learn the *Daśagranthas*, the ten books, which consist of (1) the *Saṃhitā* or the hymns; (2) the *Brāhmaṇa*, the prose treatise on sacrifices, etc.; (3) the *Āraṇyaka*, the forest-book; (4) the *Gṛihya-Sūtras*, the rules on domestic ceremonies; (5–10) the six *Angas*, treatises on pronunciation, astronomy, ceremonial, grammar, etymology, and metre. A pupil studies every day during the eight years, except on the holidays, the so-called *anadhyāya*, *i.e.* non-reading days. To complete the work in eight years he would have to learn about 12 ślokas of 32 syllables each every day.' Professor R. G. Bhandarkar is also quoted with regard to the wonderful arrangements which the Brāhmans devised for the accurate preservation of the sacred text. These were far more complicated than anything the Massoretes ever dreamed of. In the *saṃhitā* arrangement the words were in their natural order and joined together according to the Sanskrit rules of

[1] *Lectures on the Origin of Religion*, ch. iii.

[2] *Ibid.*

sandhi. In the *pada* arrangement the words were separate, that is, not united by *sandhi*, and the compounds also dissolved. In the *krama* arrangement the words were in the following order: 1, 2; 2, 3; 3, 4; 4, 5, etc., with *sandhi* between them. In the *jaṭa* arrangement the order was 1, 2, 2, 1, 1, 2; 2, 3, 3, 2, 2, 3; 3, 4, 4, 3, 3, 4, etc. In the *ghana*, 1, 2, 2, 1, 1, 2, 3, 3, 2, 1, 1, 2, 3; 2, 3, 3, 2, 2, 3, 4, 4, 3, 2, 2, 3, etc. This was, no doubt, a later development, but it must have greatly added to the burden upon the pupil's power of memorizing, which even before was almost too heavy to be borne, and we must wonder however pupils could have been willing to submit to the monotonous task of learning by rote such an enormous mass of material. It certainly seems as though the powers of memorizing gained by this laborious process have been inherited by later generations, for it is no uncommon thing for a boy in India, even at the present day, to commit on his own initiative a whole text-book to memory, a task which most English boys would find unbearable.

To get a picture of how the task of rote-learning was carried on at least 500 B.C., we can refer to the *Prātiśākhya* of the *Ṛigveda*. This work is considered to belong to the fifth or sixth century B.C., that is, to about the same time as some of the earliest of the Sūtras. Max Müller, quoting this work,[1] says—

'In the fifteenth chapter there is a description of the method followed in the schools of ancient India. The teacher, we are told, must himself have passed through the recognized curriculum and have fulfilled all the duties of a Brāhmanical student (*brahmachārī*) before he is allowed to become a teacher, and he must teach such students only as submit to all the rules of studentship. He shall settle down in a proper place. If he has only one pupil or two, they should sit on his right side; if more, they must sit as there is room for

[1] *Lectures on the Origin of Religion*, p. 159.

them. At the beginning of each lecture the pupils embrace the feet of their teacher and say, Read, Sir. The teacher answers, *Ōm*, Yes, and then pronounces two words, or if it is a compound, one. When the teacher has pronounced one word, or two, the first pupil repeats the first word; but if there is anything that requires explanation, the pupil says, Sir; and after it has been explained to him (the teacher says) *Ōm*, Yes, Sir. In this manner they go on till they have finished a *praśna* (question) which consists of three verses, or if they are verses of more than 40 to 42 syllables, of two verses. If they are *pankti* verses of 40 to 42 syllables each, a *praśna* may comprise either two or three; and if a hymn consists of one verse only, that is supposed to form a *praśna*. After the *praśna* is finished, they have all to repeat it once more, and then to go on learning it by heart, pronouncing every syllable with the high accent. After the teacher has first told a *praśna* to his pupil on the right, the others go round him to the right, and this goes on till the whole *adhyāya* or lecture is finished; a lecture consisting generally of 60 *praśnas*. At the end of the last half-verse the teacher says, Sir, and the pupil replies, *Ōm*, Yes, Sir, repeating also the verses required at the end of a lecture. The pupils then embrace the feet of their teacher, and are dismissed. The *Prātiśākhya* contains a number of minute rules besides as to repetition of words, etc.'

Besides the actual memorizing of the sacred books, we see that the teacher was in the habit of giving explanations when required by the pupil. We cannot say what this amounted to in the first place. In the case of the sacred books themselves many pupils were perhaps content simply to absorb their contents without fully understanding their meaning,[1] but when other subjects and sciences arose it would seem probable that explanation must have been given a much larger place. The *Sūtras* were composed in language so condensed

[1] But see also p. 17 above as to the *Brāhmaṇas*.

that a considerable amount of explanation must have been necessary, and they were studied together with a commentary. In the *Upanishads* we find that the philosophic teaching given there is often illustrated by parables from nature, or stories like that of Nachiketas visiting the abode of the dead. And in later works like the *Panchatantra* and the *Hitopadeśa* we find stories and fables given a very important place in the inculcation of moral truths. India is, in fact, the home of fable and allegory. If the Brāhman teachers, as seems likely, made use of this form of teaching in instructing their pupils, there must have been something at least to interest and to relieve the monotony of the laborious process of learning by heart. The system of teaching was individual, and each pupil was separately instructed by the teacher, though there may have been occasions when the teacher explained something to all the pupils at the same time. There is a passage in Manu [1] which seems to imply that the son of the teacher sometimes helped his father by teaching in his father's stead, and perhaps from this arose the custom which we find in vogue in later times of the teacher being assisted in his work by some of the older pupils who acted as monitors. When the Brāhmanic system of education first arose writing was unknown in India, but later on, when writing came into use, the task of teaching it was added to the work of the teacher.

We have seen that the Brahmanic education started out with the idea of the teacher passing on to the pupil the traditions he had himself received, and this involved primarily the learning by heart of the sacred books, but even from the earliest times the content of the education must have begun to widen out. The sacrificial ritual itself gave birth to some of the sciences. The elaborate rules for the construction of altars led to the sciences of geometry and algebra being developed, and as it was sometimes desired to erect a round altar covering

[1] Manu, ii. 208.

the same area as a square one, problems like squaring the circle had to be faced.[1] The desire to find out propitious times and seasons for sacrifice and other purposes gave rise to astrology, from which astronomy developed. The dissection of sacrificial victims was the beginning of anatomy. The care taken to preserve the sacred text from corruption led to the development of grammar and philology, while the deep questions with regard to the universe and man's place in it, which were already being referred to in the *Saṃhitās* of the Vedas, and discussed more fully in the *Āraṇyakas* and *Upanishads*, led to the formation of elaborate philosophical systems and the study of logic. Medicine also received an early development in India as well as law.

Reference has already been made to the *Sūtras*. These are the characteristic Indian text-books, and a great many were written on all sorts of subjects. According to the traditional Brāhman view there are six subjects, the study of which is necessary for the reading, understanding, or sacrificial employment of the Veda.[2] These are called the *Vedāngas*, or 'members of the Veda' They comprise the following subjects—*Śikshā* (or phonetics); *Chhandas* (or metre); *Vyākaraṇa* (or grammar); *Nirukta* (etymology or explanation of words): *Jyotisha* (or astronomy); and *Kalpa* (or ceremonial and religious practice). From these, however, other subjects developed, as, for example, the study of law from Kalpa.

The study of grammar must have been taken up in India from very early times.[3] *Pāṇini*, who is still the greatest recognized authority, was a native of Gandhāra in the northwest of India. He wrote his great grammatical work about the fourth century B.C., but refers to no less than sixty-four

[1] R. C. Dutt, *Ancient India*, pp. 93 ff.

[2] Max Müller, *Sans. Lit.*, p. 109.

[3] See *Miscellaneous Essays*, H. T. Colebrooke (ed. 1873), ii. 33 ff.; Macdonell, *Sans. Lit.*, pp. 430 ff.

predecessors. His *Sūtras* containing the rules of grammar were in eight books, called the *Ashṭādhyāyi*, comprising about four thousand aphorisms. With regard to his work Max Müller says that in grammar there is no more comprehensive collection and classification of all the facts of a language than we find in Pāṇini's *Sūtras*.[1] Pāṇini was followed in the third century B.C. by *Kātyāyana*, who wrote *Vārttikas*, or notes on some of Pāṇini's rules. Somewhat later came the *Mahābhāshya*, or great commentary, of *Patanjali*, which dates from about the second century B.C. These writers are the standard authorities on Sanskrit grammar, from whom there is, to Hindus, no appeal. Other authorities may be admitted where these writers are silent; but a deviation, even by an ancient writer, from their rules is considered a poetical licence or a barbarism. There have been many grammatical works written in India since these early writers, but they are all based on their work, and to this day the *Sūtras* of Pāṇini are committed to memory by students of Sanskrit in India. Lexicography was also cultivated in India at an early date, and the Sanskrit dictionaries are versified. The *Amarakośa*, a metrical lexicon of Sanskrit words, was composed about 500 A.D., and is still committed to memory by Indian children. The Indian phonetics of the fifth century B.C. are such an accurate analysis of the elements of language that modern ages have had much to learn from them.

There were many early writers on astronomy in India, and their works were reduced to a concise and practical form by *Āryabhaṭa*,[2] who was born at Pāṭaliputra, or Patna, in 476 A.D. He taught the rotation of the earth on its axis, and explained the causes of the eclipses of the sun and moon. Another famous Indian astronomer was Bhāskarāchārya, who was born in 1114 A.D. Closely allied to astronomy was mathematics,

[1] *Lects. on Origin of Religion*, ch. iii.

[2] Macdonell, *Sans. Lit.*, pp. 434, 435.

which is also dealt with in their works by early Indian astronomers. Algebra was also known, and it is to India that the West is indebted for its system of numerical notation, which came from India through the Arabs, and is often wrongly attributed to them. In some subjects, as, for example, astronomy, Indian scholars were influenced by Greek learning, but the exact connection in all subjects has not been fully worked out.

As the materials for the study of the subjects included in the six *Angas* increased and accumulated, such an enormous amount of matter would have to be worked through by intending students that it evidently became impossible for one student to acquire a mastery of all subjects, and so special schools arose for the study of special subjects.[1] In the Vedic schools the chief object was to acquire a complete mastery of the sacred text, and this in itself was a huge task even if only one Veda were attempted. At first the *Angas* were no doubt short treatises, but in course of time they grew enormously in bulk. Grammar, for example, was developed by Pāṇini and others, and their works became in themselves voluminous. Other sciences also came to be developed. If a student aimed at committing all the Vedic texts to memory, together with the accompanying *Angas*, he might succeed in his task, but he could hardly have gained a real understanding of the subject-matter. He became simply a kind of walking library.

It must have become necessary at some time for those who wished to become masters of separate subjects to restrict the number of works which were learned by heart and specialize in some part of the field of knowledge. This is made clear by the state of Hindu learning in India in modern times. It is said that there are men called Vaidiks who can recite whole volumes of the sacred texts. But besides this there are

[1] For the beginnings of specialization, see Bühler, *S.B.E.*, vol. xxv. pp. xlvi. ff.

specialists who have an expert knowledge of some part of the ancient learning, such as the performance of sacrifices, grammar, law, or astronomy. This specialization must have begun in very early times, as the work of the grammarians like Pāṇini shows. Thus were formed special schools for various subjects, which included grammar, law, and astronomy. This specialization began probably about the fifth century B.C. It is thought that law became a special subject of study at a somewhat later date than grammar or astronomy, but even in some of the *Dharma Sūtras* (*Vasishṭha* and *Baudhāyana*) there are traces that the specialization had already begun. The *Mānava Dharmaśāstra*. or Law Code of Manu, grew up in one of these special law schools.

The science of medicine also was developed in India at an early date.[1] One of the great authorities was Charaka, and he is said by a Chinese authority to have been the court physician of the Buddhist King Kanishka in the first century of our era. Another great name is that of Suśruta. who lived about the fourth or fifth century A.D. It is probable that the development of medical science owed something to the influence of Buddhism, with its strong regard for the sacredness of life and insistence on the law of kindness. Through Arabic channels Indian medical science had a great influence on the subject as studied and practised in Europe in the Middle Ages, and even in the eighteenth century the operation of rhinoplasty was borrowed from India by European surgery. Hindu physicians are called *Vaidyas*, and *Āyur-Vedic* medicine, as it is named, is still practised in India.

In philosophy we can trace the beginnings of the subject right back to the *Upanishads*, and even to the *Brāhmaṇas* and *Saṃhitās*. The six recognized systems or schools of philosophy began to develop before the beginning of the Christian era, and are in three pairs, each pair having close connection.

[1] Macdonell, *Sans. Lit.*, pp. 435, 436.

The *Pūrvamīmāṃsā* and the *Uttaramīmāṃsā* (or *Vedānta*) represent orthodox Brāhman thought. The former teaches the eternity of the Veda and explains the meaning and value of the 'Way of Works', especially of sacrificial acts. The latter expounds the 'Way of Knowledge', and teaches that the All, or Brahman, alone truly exists and is one, and the soul is Brahman. The subject is synthesized with the object, '*Tat tvam asi*' ('Thou art That'). The *Sānkhya* philosophy is atheistic, and teaches a species of dualism, and that salvation, or release from matter, is attained by a clear knowledge of the distinction between soul and matter. The *Yoga* is closely connected with the *Sānkhya*, but postulates a personal God, and advocates an elaborate system of postures and ascetic exercises as helpful in enabling the soul to reach the highest truth. The *Nyāya* philosophy deals with logic, but it is not so much a treatise of formal logic as an exposition of the way that salvation can be attained by the removal of false knowledge. The *Vaiśeshika* presupposes a knowledge of the *Nyāya*, and often goes over the same ground. It contains a theory of atoms. The smallest and invisible particles are eternal in themselves, but not eternal as aggregates.

From the most ancient times there existed in India Brāhmanic settlements, and in connection with them *parishads*, or assemblies of learned Brāhmans, which gave decisions on all points connected with the Brāhmanic religion and learning.[1] In the *Bṛihadāraṇyaka Upanishad* we read that Śvetaketu went to the *parishad* of the Panchālas.[2] Max Müller says[3] that according to modern writers a *parishad* ought to consist of twenty-one Brāhmans, well versed in philosophy, theology, and law. But in early periods it seems that a smaller number was sufficient. Gautama says[4] that a *parishad* shall consist of at

[1] R. C. Dutt, *Ancient India*.

[2] *Bṛih. Ār. Up.*, vi. 2.

[3] Max Müller, *Sans. Lit.*, pp. 128–132.

[4] Gautama, xxviii. 48–51.

least the ten following members, namely, four men who have completely studied the four Vedas, three men belonging to the three orders enumerated first, and three men who know different institutes of law. In *Vasishṭha*[1] and *Baudhāyana* it is said that it shall consist of four men who each know one of the four Vedas, a student of the *Mīmāṃsā*, one who knows the *Angas*, one who recites the works on the sacred law, and three Brāhmans belonging to three different orders. The regulations in Manu are as follows[2]:—

'If it is asked how it should be with respect to points of the law which have not been specially mentioned, the answer is, that which Brāhmans who are Śishṭas propound, shall doubtlessly have legal force. Those Brāhmans must be considered as Śishṭas who, in accordance with the sacred law, have studied the Veda together with its appendages, and are able to adduce proofs perceptible by the senses from the revealed texts. Whatever an assembly, consisting either of at least ten, or of at least three persons who follow their prescribed occupations, declares to be law, the legal force of that one must not dispute. Three persons who each know one of the three principal Vedas, a logician, a Mīmāṃsaka, one who knows the *Nirukta*, one who recites the Institutes of the sacred law, and three men belonging to the first three orders, shall constitute a legal assembly, consisting of at least ten members. One who knows the *Ṛigveda*, one who knows the *Yajurveda*, and one who knows the *Sāmaveda*, shall be known to form an assembly consisting of at least three members and competent to decide doubtful points of law. Even that which one Brāhman versed in the Veda declares to be law must be considered to have supreme legal force, but not that which is proclaimed by myriads of ignorant men.'

The ideal in ancient times thus seems to have been that

[1] *Vas.* iii. 20; *Baudh.* i. 1, 5–13.
[2] Manu, xii. 108–113.

the *parishad* should consist of at least ten persons, but a smaller number might be regarded as sufficient in case of necessity. Thus *Parāśara*, another ancient authority,[1] says that 'four or even three able men from amongst the Brāhmans in a village, who know the Veda and keep the sacrificial fire, form a *parishad*. Or if they do not keep the sacrificial fire, five or three who have studied the Vedas and the Vedāngas, and know the law, may well form a *parishad*. Of old sages who possess the highest knowledge of the divine self, who are twice-born, perform sacrifices, and have purified themselves in the duties of the Veda, one also may be considered as a *parishad*.'

The composition of this assembly is interesting as showing how specialization in Vedic study had begun in very early times. Thus in Gautama, besides the four men who have completely studied the Veda—that is, men of the walking library type—there are those who know the different *Dharma Sūtras*, besides the three representatives of the orders. In *Vasishṭha* and *Baudhāyana* the three specialists are a student of the *Mīmāṃsā*, that is, one who knows the sacrificial rules, one who knows the *Angas*, and one who recites the works on the sacred law. In Manu those who know the Vedas are reduced to three, and the specialists are a logician, a Mīmāṃsaka, one who knows the *Nirukta*, and one who recites the Institutes of the sacred law. No doubt the exact composition of the *parishad* may have varied in different places, but the growth of specialization in studies seems to be clearly shown. The representatives of the three orders were a student, a householder, and a hermit, or according to some authorities a student, a householder, and an ascetic.

These *parishads* were in some respects like judicial assemblies, and in others like ecclesiastical synods, but as those who composed them were most of them also teachers,

[1] Quoted by Max Müller, *Sans. Lit.*, pp. 128–132.

they correspond to a certain extent to the associations of teachers in the Middle Ages of Europe which developed into universities. Thus not only were different faculties represented, but even a student was a member of the *parishad.* The settlement of Brāhmans proficient in different branches of the ancient learning in various centres must have meant the gathering together also of a number of students who were receiving instruction from them, and thus these *parishads* would form the nucleus of something corresponding to a university.

This would be specially the case in some places where a large number of Brāhman teachers were gathered together, like towns or monastic institutions. An instance of an early Brāhmanic intellectual centre is Takshaśilā (or Taxilā). This was the capital of Gandhāra in North-West India, the native land of Pāṇini, the grammarian, and its site is not far from the modern Rawalpindi. It was a stronghold of Brāhmanic learning as early as the fourth or fifth century B.C. and perhaps earlier. Here at the time of Alexander's invasion the Greeks first came into contact with the Brāhman philosophers, and were astonished at their asceticism and strange doctrines. Many other centres of learning, as, for example, Benares, and Nadiā, became famous in later times. In the Buddhist system of education it was the monastery, as will be shown, which was the centre of learning. Monasteries have never had such an important place in Hinduism as in Buddhism, but they have existed, and are still to be found. Among the most famous are the monasteries or *maṭhas* founded by the great Vedāntist scholar Śankarāchārya [1] (born *circ.* 788 A.D.) at Sringeri, Badari, Dwaraka, and Puri. These institutions are still in existence.[2] The most celebrated of them is

[1] Śankarāchārya was an exponent of the *Advaita,* or extreme monistic form of Vedānta philosophy.

[2] See *Śrī Śankarāchārya, His Life and Times,* by C. N. Krishnaswamy Aiyar, pp. 67-84.

Sringeri in the Mysore state. Though primarily religious institutions they give attention to the study of Sanskrit and of logic and the Vedānta philosophy.

A development of the relation between teacher and pupil, which has already been sketched, was the exaltation of the teacher to such a position of reverence that he was worshipped by his pupil.[1] In the schools of the early Vedānta the teacher, or *guru*, was always one who was himself supposed to have reached emancipation, and thus to have come to the realization that he is Brāhman. In his devotion, or *bhakti*, for Brāhman it was but a short step for the pupil to feel *bhakti* also for the *guru*, who was thus identified with Brāhman. This is referred to as early as the *Śvetāśvatara Upanishad*[2] (perhaps about the fourth century B.C.), but it received a great emphasis in all the chief *bhakti* sects (Vaishṇava, Śaiva, or other) from at least the seventh century A.D. In these the disciple is taught to worship his *guru* as God. This was of course an honour paid to a religious teacher, but it had an effect upon the relation of all pupils and teachers, and helps to explain the high respect which students of to-day have even for a teacher of secular subjects.

Brāhmanic education has continued from very early times right down to the present day, and throughout that long period, though there was some development and change, its salient features have remained the same. The long struggle with Buddhism ended in a triumph for the Brāhmans, but not without their own system becoming modified, but it had little influence on the educational system. The rule of the Muhammadans was, on the whole, unfavourable towards Brāhman learning, although it was patronized by Akbar and others. Some of the more ruthless, or more orthodox, of Muhammadan sovereigns destroyed Brāhman places of

[1] See Farquhar, *Crown of Hinduism*, p. 402.
[2] *Śvetāś. Up.*, vi. 23

learning, and scattered their students, but in spite of this interruption Brāhman learning continued.

Throughout the centuries since the *Sūtras* were written the history of Brāhmanic education is difficult to trace. There was probably very little development with regard to either theory or practice, and the subjects of the curriculum remained very much the same. The development of monastic institutions, and of *guru* worship, has already been referred to. In the Buddhist period the Brāhmanic learning continued side by side with the Buddhist. The latter was indeed largely influenced both in its ideals and practice by the Brāhmanic education, and borrowed many of its text-books from the Brāhmans, especially when the Buddhists adopted Sanskrit as a vehicle of instruction. The educational institutions of the Buddhists, like Nālanda, were at one period probably more influential and popular than those of the Brāhmans. When the Muhammadan invasions burst upon India both Brāhman and Buddhist educational institutions suffered severely, and those of the Buddhists gradually decayed and disappeared, a process which was helped by the assimilation of Buddhism in India with Hinduism. But the Brāhman education continued in spite of difficulties, and as the Buddhist centres of learning decayed those of the Brāhmans became more prominent.

Brāhman schools of Sanskrit learning were indeed scattered all over the land in numerous towns and villages. These institutions were known as *tols*. Sometimes in a town of special sanctity, or even of political importance, numbers of these *tols* were established side by side and constituted a kind of university. Examples of these are Benares and Nadiā.

Nadiā, or Navadvīpa ('New Island'), was a town founded in 1063 A.D. by one of the Sen kings of Bengal.[1] In 1203 it was captured by the Muhammadans. From the earliest days

[1] See *Nadiā Gazetteer* (*Bengal District Gazetteers*, No. 24), 1910, pp. 180 ff.; also *Adam's Reports*, pp. 49 ff.

the patronage of its Hindu rulers and its political importance, as well as also the sanctity of the site, attracted a large number of scholars who taught the Brāhmanic learning to thousands of students, and this continued even when Nadiā lost its political importance. Among erudite teachers who taught in Nadiā are Abdihodha Yogi, a pandit who is said to have founded there the first school of logic; a subject for which Nadiā has since been specially famous. Bāsudev Sarbabhauma, another of its famous savants, is said, while a pupil of Pakshādhar Misra, the first logician of Mithilā, to have learnt by heart the whole of the treatise on logic. Among his distinguished pupils were Raghunāth Siromani, the author of the *Didhiti*, and the commentary on the *Gautama Sūtra;* Raghunandana Smarta Bhatacharya, the most renowned teacher of law in Bengal, whose school is followed even to this day throughout the whole province; Krishnananda Agambagis, whose work on Tantra philosophy is the standard book on the subject; and Gauranga, or Chaitanya, the leader of a great Vaishṇava sect in the sixteenth century.

A *tol* consists generally of a thatched chamber in which the pandit and the class meet, and a collection of mud hovels round a quadrangle, in which the students live in the simplest manner. Each student has his own hut, in which there is scarcely any furniture except his brass water-pot and mat. A student remains at the *tol* often for eight or ten years, according to whether he is studying law or logic. The pandit does not always live at the *tol*, but comes every day on which study takes place, from an early hour till sunset. The huts are built and repaired at his expense. No fees are charged, and until recent years the pandit even helped to provide his pupils with food and clothing. He himself obtained the necessary funds by grants and by the presents which his fame as a teacher ensured to him at religious ceremonies. The usual number of students in a *tol* is about twenty-five, though there may be more. These, in most cases, have no means of subsistence. The teacher provides them with shelter and free tuition, and food and clothes they obtain from him and also from shopkeepers and landholders and by begging at the chief festivals.

At Nadiā the chief study is logic, but law and grammar are also taught. Dialectical discussions are frequently held, and the ambition of the student is to gain success at one of these discussions held at a festival, and by adroit and hair-splitting arguments to silence his opponent. Professor Cowell, who visited the schools at Nadiā in 1867, says:[1] 'I could not help looking at these unpretending lecture-halls with a deep interest, as I thought of the pandits lecturing there to generation after generation of eager, inquisitive minds. Seated on the floor with his "corona" of listening pupils round him, the teacher expatiates on those refinements of infinitesimal logic which make a European's brain dizzy to think of, but whose labyrinth a trained Nadiā student will thread with unfaltering precision. I noticed during my visit middle-aged and even grey-haired men among the students.'

The number of *tols* and of students at Nadiā seems to have fluctuated considerably. In 1816 there were said to be 46 schools and 380 pupils; but in 1818, Ward estimated 31 schools only, but as many as 747 students; and in 1829 H. H. Wilson found about 500 to 600 pupils. The numbers for more recent years are as follows: In 1864, 12 *tols* and 150 pupils; in 1881, 20 *tols* and 100 pupils; in 1901, 40 *tols* and 274 pupils; in 1908, 30 *tols* and 250 pupils. Of the 31 schools which Ward found, 17 studied logic, 11 studied law, and the other 3 poetry, astronomy, and grammar respectively.

William Ward gives us[2] some interesting sidelights on

[1] Quoted in *Nadiā Gazetteer*, p. 182.

[2] Ward, ii. 483 ff.

Brāhmanic education as he found it, especially in Bengal, at the beginning of the nineteenth century. He says that Hindu colleges or schools were called 'Chutooshpathee', that is, the place where four śāstras were studied. These four were grammar, law, the *purāṇas*, and the *darśanas* (or philosophy). This word was corrupted to 'Chouparee'. The places of learning were usually built of clay, and consisted sometimes of three rooms and sometimes of eight or ten, in two rows, with a reading-room open on all sides at the farther end. These huts were frequently erected at the expense of the teacher, who not only solicited alms to raise the building, but also to feed his pupils. Ward says that three kinds of Brāhmanic schools existed in Bengal. In the first, grammar and poetry as well as the *purāṇas* and *smṛitis* were studied; in the second kind the law works and the *purāṇas*; and in the third the *Nyāya Darśana*, or logic. Select works were read and explained, but there was no instruction by lectures. The lessons were committed to memory and then explained by the teacher. In other parts of India, he says, colleges were not common, but individuals at their houses taught grammar, and mendicant Brāhmans taught the Vedas and other Śāstras at the *maṭhas*, or monastic institutions, where they rested. No fees were received from the pupils, but they received presents from them. Unless patronized by a rich man the subsistence of the teacher was in most cases a scanty one. Pupils were generally over twelve years of age, and were generally maintained by their parents, and resided either at the college or at the house of some neighbour. In Benares Ward found 83 *maṭhas* and 1371 pupils. The average number of pupils to each teacher was 16 or 17. Some of these schools studied the Veda, some only grammar, some studied poetry, some the Vedānta, some logic and law, and some astronomy. Ward also gives lists of schools at Nadiā and Calcutta, and mentions many other places where Sanskrit schools existed.

With regard to libraries, he says that some colleges contained as many as ten, and others as many as forty or fifty volumes. Like students in other parts of the world these Brāhmanic pupils were not always ideal in their behaviour, and Ward mentions their extravagance, night frolics, robbing of orchards, and other misdemeanours. With regard to the motives which led to pupils undergoing this form of education, he says that learned Brāhmans were more esteemed by the Hindus than ignorant ones, and received more costly presents. Offices under Government also were open to those Brāhmans who had a knowledge of the ancient law. Moreover, those who were going to perform the priestly rites for Hindu families needed at least some knowledge of Hindu learning.

With regard to the old Brāhmanic education as it exists in India to-day, the last Quinquennial Review of Education in India states [1] that in 1912 there existed 1178 private Sanskrit schools. Most of these would be schools of the old type. They had decreased from 1630 in 1907. Mr. de la Fosse, speaking of the United Provinces, is quoted as saying,[2] 'Sanskrit *pāthshālas* of the indigenous type . . . are, generally speaking, rather poorly attended. They are to be found where the number of the Brāhman population is sufficient to create a demand for the learning of a little Sanskrit and Hindu astrology. The pupils seem to spend their time in casting horoscopes, or divining auspicious days and times for commencing occupations. The schools may be classed as professional, for the scholars are destined to earn their livelihood by presiding at or helping in the performance of those religious ceremonies which make up so large a part of the life of the orthodox Hindu villager. In some a little Hindi is taught and also writing, but not much attention is paid to this side of the work.'

At the present time the spread of education on Western

[1] Vol. ii. p. 289. [2] Vol. i. p. 272.

lines has meant that the majority even of Brāhman youths who wish for an education that will give them the opportunity of obtaining good employment have forsaken the old system of learning; but it is still to be found, although the extent of its operations has been considerably curtailed. It is rare indeed to find those who pass through all the four stages of student, householder, hermit, and wandering ascetic; but it is interesting to find that not only does the rite of initiation still take place, but that it preserves some at least of the features of early times in its outward ceremonies. Thus [1] in the performance of the ceremony in some parts of India to-day, it is the custom to light a sacred fire which is kept alight during the days that the ceremony lasts and is fed with the twigs of certain trees. The father of the youth takes the place of the teacher, and when the sacred cord is put on, it has attached to it a bit of skin of a deer, if procurable. This seems to be a relic of the old custom of Brāhmanic students wearing certain skins as part of their dress. After the initiation the father at once proceeds to teach the boy the *gāyatrī* prayer, and after initiation the novice begins to ask alms of those present. He is also instructed during these days in the morning, midday, and evening prayers and other ceremonies. Thus the initiation of the *brahmachārī* is still carried out very much as it was in India more than two thousand five hundred years ago, though it is not, except in a few cases, followed by the actual study of the Vedas and the accompanying sciences.

In ancient times probably most Brāhmans passed through the period of studentship, but they did not necessarily all become teachers, and in Manu certain other occupations are admitted as allowable for a Brāhman. With regard to Kshatriyas and Vaiśyas, who were also eligible for studentship, it is impossible to say how many of them really undertook the responsibilities of this position. As shown elsewhere, it is

[1] J. E. Padfield, *The Hindu at Home*, pp. 68 ff.

probable that for them the study of the Veda was something far less serious than for young Brāhmans, and the duties which they had to perform in life must have necessitated their receiving the education suitable for their special callings before they became adults. Probably they tended less and less to attend the Brāhmanic schools, and vocational schools, or at least domestic training, for their future duties in life were developed. The Śūdras were always shut out from Brāhmanic education, and they also developed their own system of training for the young craftsman. The popular system of education, which will be noticed in a later chapter, also grew up to meet a need for which the Brāhmanic schools made no provision.

Some of the ideals of the ancient Brāhmanic education will be discussed further in a separate chapter, as well as the causes of its decline, but reviewing it briefly as a whole, one may say that, like the Muhammadan education with which it has many points of similarity, it was at least not inferior to the education of Europe before the Revival of Learning. Not only did the Brāhman educators develop a system of education which survived the crumbling of empires and the changes of society, but they also, through all these thousands of years, kept aglow the torch of higher learning, and numbered amongst them many great thinkers who have left their mark not only upon the learning of India, but upon the intellectual life of the world.

CHAPTER II

THE EDUCATION OF SOME SPECIAL CLASSES OF THE COMMUNITY

THE early Vedic schools for the training of priests seem to have been confined to the youths of the priestly class, and the Brāhmans kept in their families the ancient literature which formed the basis of all higher education. Even in quite early times, however, it is evident that some of the non-Brāhmans attained to a high degree of notoriety as men of wisdom. There is, for example, a certain king Janaka, of Videha,[1] who is referred to in the *Brāhmaṇas* and the *Upanishads* as gaining distinction in debates with learned Brāhmans. Other royal sages also are mentioned, like Chitra Gāngyāyani [2] and Ajātaśatru,[3] who were able to give Brāhmans instruction on deep questions of philosophy. In early days such instruction as the young Kshatriyas and Vaiśyas received would presumably be given by their fathers and confined to teaching them the duties of their particular calling in life. It probably marks the growing power of the Brāhmans that at some time the training of the young Kshatriyas and Vaiśyas came into their hands, and it became the exclusive privilege of the Brāhman caste to give instruction. Even at the time when the hymns of the *Ṛigveda* were being composed it was the custom for the chieftains or nobles to have a Brāhman as a

[1] *Śatapatha Brāhmaṇa*, xi. 6, 2, 10.
[2] *Kaushītaki Up.*, i.
[3] *Bṛih. Ār. Up.*, ii. 1

domestic priest or chaplain, called a *purohita*,[1] and it is easy to see how the instruction of the sons of his patron would come under his care, and that this system would gradually be extended to all the Aryan youth as the power of the Brāhman priesthood increased.

By the time that the earliest *Dharmasūtras* which are extant were composed (*circa* 500 B.C.) the system was in full working order, and it had become customary[2] for Kshatriyas and Vaiśyas, as well as for Brāhmans, to be initiated with the sacred thread as a preliminary to entering upon the period of school life under Brāhman teachers, which was to occupy at least twelve years. The difference in the time of initiation, and of dress to be worn by the three 'twice-born' castes, has already been referred to in the previous chapter.[3] The later age at which the Kshatriyas and Vaiśyas were supposed to start their schooling must be taken to indicate that its character was for them somewhat different from the instruction which the young Brāhman received. The latter was at school to be prepared for his future vocation as a priest and a teacher, and much that he would require to know would not only be useless to the youths of the other castes, but it is not likely that the Brāhmans would wish to communicate all the mysteries of their priestly office to them. For the Kshatriyas and Vaiśyas, 'studying the Veda' must have meant much less than for the Brāhmans. It may have included the memorizing of the Vedic hymns, and an acquaintance with the philosophic teaching of the *Upanishads*, and certain parts of the six *Angas*, such as were necessary for the understanding of the Vedic texts, or for an acquaintance with duties to be performed in their subsequent life. It was also for them, as well as for the Brāhmans, regarded as a time of *āśrama* or discipline, and a stage in the preparation for the life after death.

[1] *Ṛigveda*, i. 1.

[2] Gautama, i.; Āpast., i. 1.

[3] See pp. 28 ff.

Warriors.—It seems most likely that as time went on the 'study of the Veda' for the Kshatriyas and Vaiśyas became still more attenuated, and that their education was more and more confined to those subjects which had a more direct bearing on their future calling. It has been shown in the previous chapter how the special schools of law, grammar, etc., began to grow out of the six *Angas*, somewhere about the fifth century B.C. The *Dharmasūtras* are connected with *kalpa*,[1] and they contain not only the beginnings of law afterwards developed in the *Dharmaśāstras*, but also instruction on the duties of the king. This was no doubt the germ of the science of politics which was afterwards developed in the works known as *Nītiśāstras* and *Arthaśāstras*.

In the *Dharmasūtras* of Āpastamba, Baudhāyana, and Vasishṭha there is no mention of the subjects to be studied by the king, but in Gautama[2] it is said that he shall be 'fully instructed in the threefold sacred science and in logic'.[3] It further says[4] that the administration of justice shall be by the Veda, the *Dharmaśāstra*,[5] the *Angas*, and the *Purāṇa*,[6] so that it may be presumed that the royal princes were expected to become acquainted with these also during their period of schooling. A knowledge of the use of arms and of military skill was, of course, necessary, and a great deal of the time of the young Kshatriyas must have been given to learning their duties as warriors. Already in the hymns of the *Ṛigveda* there is a passage[7] which appears to refer to military combats

[1] *I.e.* 'ceremonial and religious practices' (see p. 42).

[2] Gautama, xi. 1.

[3] *Ibid.*, xi. 3. The word translated 'logic' is *ānvīkshikī*, as in *Arthaśāstra*, ii. (see p. 63).

[4] Gautama, xi. 19.

[5] Bühler considers this word as probably an interpolation, for it was included in the *Angas* as part of *Kalpa.*

[6] *Purāṇa*, *i.e.* ancient legendary tales.

[7] *Ṛigveda*, iv. 42, 5.

amongst young warriors, and as the Kshatriyas became marked off from the other castes as those whose function it was to fight for their protection, the practice of arms must have become more highly specialized. In the *Mahābhārata*[1] we read[2] how the young Pāṇḍu and Kuru princes were instructed in the various kinds of military skill. This included fighting on horseback and on elephants, in chariots and on the ground. The weapons used were the club, the sword, the lance, the spear, the dart, and above all the bow. The preceptor of these young princes in the use of arms is said to have been not, as we might have supposed, a Kshatriya warrior, but a learned Brāhman named Droṇa. The purpose of the author may have been to exalt the dignity of the Brāhman caste by showing how the Kshatriyas learned even their own special functions from the Brāhmans. In the *Rāmāyaṇa*[3] of Vālmīki we read with regard to Rāma and his brothers[4]—

'And among all those princes, the eldest, Rāma, like unto Ketu, and the special delight of his father, became the object of general regard, even as the self-create Himself. And all of them were versed in the Vedas, and heroic, and intent upon the welfare of others. And all were accomplished in knowledge, and endowed with virtues, and among them all, the exceedingly puissant Rāma, having truth for prowess, was the desire of every one, and spotless like unto the Moon himself. He could ride on elephants and horses, and was an adept in managing cars (chariots), and he was ever engaged in the study of arms and aye occupied in ministering unto his sire. . . . Those best of men, ever engaged in the study of the Vedas, were accomplished in the art of archery, and always intent upon ministering unto their father.'

[1] The original germ of this epic dates from about the fifth century B.C., but it contains vast additions of post-Christian times.

[2] M. N. Dutt's translation, pp. 190 f.

[3] Original germ *circa* 500 B.C.

[4] M. N. Dutt's translation, *Bālakāndam*, pp. 51 f.

This extract brings out what seem to be the chief aims of education in the case of the young Kshatriyas in early times, namely, the study of the Vedas, military skill, and right moral conduct. There is no mention of any other special training for the performance of their royal duties, but silence in a work of this kind is of little value as evidence.

At some time, however, between 500 B.C. and the rise of the Mauryan dynasty (321 B.C.) there seems to have been a considerable development of Kshatriya education. The science of politics had grown up, and much more attention was given to fitting young princes for the duties of their high office. We have a valuable picture of this education in the *Arthaśāstra* of Kauṭilya. The number of authorities whose different opinions he quotes and sometimes refutes shows how the science of politics had developed, and amongst other things there was a considerable interest as to what was the best kind of education for a young prince to receive. It is not impossible that this development in royal education may have been a result of the desire of some Indian rulers to improve the efficiency of their kingdoms in view of the possibilities of Persian invasion from the west, for the Indus valley had been annexed and formed into a satrapy by Darius (521–485 B.C.), and the raid of Alexander (327–324 B.C.) would have stimulated this desire. But whether this was so or not, it seems certain that a considerable development of royal education took place about this period.

The *Arthaśāstra* of Kauṭilya [1] is ascribed to Kauṭilya, also known as Chānakya, the Brāhman who overthrew the Nanda dynasty and placed Chandragupta Maurya on the throne. If he was the author, the work would be dated somewhere between 321 and 296 B.C. The authenticity,[2] however, has been disputed, and the book may have been based on the

[1] Translated by Mr. R. Shāmaśāstry.
[2] For authenticity, see *Journal of Royal Asiatic Society*, 1916, p. 130.

teaching of Kauṭilya, although not by his hand, and belong in its present form perhaps to the first century B.C., while incorporating older matter. In any case it is a remarkable document, and throws a most valuable light on the system of administration and social life at the time of the Mauryan Empire. It is a manual of political science, Machiavellian in its principles, for the use of kings, and amongst other things outlines an educational programme for royal princes.

Kautilya holds [1] that there are four sciences which should be included in the royal education. These are *Ānvīkshikī*, the triple Vedas, *Vārta*, and *Daṇḍanīti*. *Ānvīkshikī* is defined as comprising the *Sānkhya*, *Yoga*, and *Lokāyata* philosophies. *Vārta* includes a knowledge of agriculture, cattle-breeding, and trade. *Daṇḍanīti* is the science of government, including a knowledge of criminal law. It seems, however, that the authorities were not agreed as to the number of the sciences to be taught, and though Kauṭilya holds that the four sciences mentioned above should be studied, he says that others held different opinions. The school of Manu (Mānava) held that philosophy was only a special branch of Vedic study, and that, therefore, there were only three sciences to be studied. The school of Bṛihaspati held that there were only two sciences, *Vārta* and *Daṇḍanīti*, for Veda study, they said, was 'only an abridgment for a man experienced in temporal affairs', which means, presumably, that a young prince or Kshatriya would not have the time to obtain more than a very casual acquaintance with the Vedas. The school of Uśanas declared that there was only one science, the science of *Daṇḍanīti*, all others having their beginning in that.

Having thus outlined the curriculum, Kauṭilya in another chapter [2] gives some further particulars with regard to his scheme of education. Although he admits four sciences as enumerated above, he says that the first three are dependent

[1] *Arthaśāstra*, ch. ii. [2] *Ibid.*, ch. v.

on *Daṇḍanīti*, for *Daṇḍa* (punishment), which alone can procure safety and security of life, is, in its turn, dependent on discipline.

'Discipline,' he says, 'is of two kinds: artificial and natural; for instruction can render only a docile being conformable to the rules of discipline, and not an undocile being. The study of sciences can tame only those who are possessed of such mental faculties as obedience, hearing, grasping, retentive memory, discrimination, inference, and deliberation, but not others devoid of such faculties.' By natural discipline he means, it would seem, the discipline which arises from the docility of the pupil; for those who have not this there is the artificial discipline of punishment.

'Sciences,' he continues, 'shall be studied, and their precepts strictly observed under the authority of specialist teachers. Having undergone the ceremony of tonsure, the student shall learn the alphabet and arithmetic. After investiture with the sacred thread, he shall study the triple Vedas, the science of *Ānvīkshikī* under teachers of acknowledged authority, the science of *Vārta* under Government superintendents, and the science of *Daṇḍanīti* under theoretical and practical politicians.'

It would seem from this that the last two studies were to be learnt in very close contact with their practice in actual life.

With regard to the length of the course we are told that 'the prince shall observe celibacy till he becomes sixteen years old. Then he shall observe the ceremony of tonsure and marry'. If the investiture with the sacred thread took place in accordance with the regulations given in the *Dharmasūtras* in the eleventh year after conception, the course would thus last six years, which is much shorter than the twelve years prescribed as necessary for the *Brahmachārī* to learn one Veda. It is, of course not impossible that the study of *Vārta* and *Daṇḍanīti* at least may have been continued even after marriage.

During the period of study the young prince was to be placed under the strict supervision of his teachers. 'In maintaining efficient discipline he shall ever and invariably keep company with aged professors of sciences in whom alone discipline has its firm root.'

The hours of study were thus planned out. 'He shall spend the forenoon in receiving lessons in military arts concerning elephants, horses, chariots, and weapons, and the afternoon in hearing the *Itihāsa*'. *Itihāsa* is said to include *Purāṇa*, *Itivṛitta* (history), *Ākhyāyika* (tales), *Udāharaṇa* (illustrative stories), *Dharmaśāstra*, and *Arthaśāstra*. The first four would include mythological and epic tales, and those moral fables and stories such as were collected (afterwards) in the *Panchatantra* and the *Hitopadeśa*.[1] The last two include what would now be termed law and political science, and would cover the theoretical parts of *Vārta* and *Daṇḍanīti*.

'During the rest of the day and nights he shall not only receive new lessons and revise old lessons, but also hear over and again what has not been clearly understood.'

It is curious that in this outline of the day's work there is no mention of the study of the Veda or philosophy. One cannot help wondering, in spite of the opinion of Kauṭilya that they should be included in the programme of studies, whether they received very serious attention in the case of the young princes.

Kauṭilya goes on to say that 'from hearing ensues knowledge; from knowledge steady application (*yoga*) is possible; and from application, self-possession (*ātmavattā*) is possible. This is what is meant by efficiency in learning (*vidyāsāmarthyam*). The king who is well educated and disciplined in

[1] See p. 68.

sciences, devoted to good government of his subjects, and bent on doing good to all people, will enjoy the earth unopposed'.

The programme of education thus outlined is by no means an unworthy scheme for the education of a young prince. It shows the wonderful powers which these early Brāhman educators had of adapting their system to the needs of the pupils, and of devising a vocational training for the sons of noble families. It is not clear whether this education was confined to those who were the scions of ruling houses or whether other young Kshatriyas shared in its advantages, but it would seem not unlikely that noble families would seek to give their sons an education at least approximating to that which princes received.

In the Law of Manu, which is considered to date, in its present form, from about 200 A.D., though based on an older *Mānava Dharma Sūtra*, it is said with regard to the education of a king,[1] 'From those versed in the three Vedas let him learn the threefold sacred science, the primeval science of government, the science of dialectics, and the knowledge of the supreme Soul, from the people the theory of the various trades and professions'. According to the *Arthaśāstra*[2] the school of Mānava held that there were three sciences to be studied, namely, the Vedas and the philosophy based on them, the science of government (*Daṇḍanīti*), and agriculture and trade (*Vārta*), so that these three are presumably covered by the subjects mentioned in the Law of Manu.

It is to be presumed that, as in the ordinary Brāhmanic study, the work was based on a knowledge of the grammar of the Sanskrit language. The story contained in the *Kathā-sarit-sāgara*[3] of the king who did not know his Sanskrit

[1] Manu, vii. 43.
[2] See p. 63.
[3] *Kathā-sarit-sāgara*, Tar. vi. 108–164.

grammar seems to show that some royal pupils did not always find it easy to master all its intricacies.

With regard to text-books those used in the ordinary Brāhman schools for Vedic study would serve also for the Kshatriyas in so far as they studied the same subjects, but there were two developments which arose to meet the needs of the special training required by them. We have already referred to the *Nītiśāstra* or *Arthaśāstra* as a manual of political science. The *Arthaśāstra* of Kauṭilya, from which we have quoted above, is an example, and there were probably many which have not survived. This *Arthaśāstra* contains a detailed account of the duties of the king and of his officials, and of the way the administration was carried on, and in connection with the work of the superintendents of different departments contains a good deal of information with regard to agriculture and trade, and thus included probably what was to be taught to the princes under the heading of *Vārta*. It also contains several chapters on the military science of those days. The *Nītisāra*, or *Essence of Conduct*, is a metrical treatise by an author named Kāmandaka. It is evidently based on the teaching of the *Artnaśāstra* of Kauṭilya, and contains in a condensed form many of the principles of policy taught in the *Arthaśāstra*. It belongs to about the third century A.D., or perhaps later. But the Brāhman preceptors, finding perhaps that their royal or noble pupils did not always take kindly to the effort of studying the political wisdom of the *Arthaśāstra*, devised the plan of using fables and stories as a vehicle for the teaching of this science. 'It[1] is a combination highly characteristic of a civilization of which the two most important features were the intellectual passion and subtlety of the Brāhman Schools on the one hand, and the village life of a humorous people on the other.' The *Panchatantra* existed in the first half of the sixth century A.D., but

[1] *J.R.A.S.*, 1910, pp. 966 ff.

the *Tantrākhyāyikā*, which is considered to be its most original and earliest form, was composed many centuries earlier.[1] It is introduced with the story of a certain king who had three particularly idle and stupid sons. He wished to find a teacher for them, and at last met with a certain Brāhman, who promised in six months to give the young princes such instruction that they should surpass all others in the knowledge of right conduct. For the accomplishment of his object he composed the *Panchatantra.* It consists of a series of fables which illustrate various points of moral conduct, and expose many human vices, like the intriguing of courtiers and the faithlessness of women. The Brāhmans themselves do not escape satire, which is levelled, for example, against their avarice and hypocrisy. The *Hitopadeśa* is a similar collection of fables, later than the *Panchatantra*, on which it is based, but the date of which is quite uncertain.[2] There are also other collections of fables like them, as, for instance, the *Kathā-sarit-sāgara.* The *Mahābhārata* contains a great deal of didactic material embedded in the story, and this may also have been used in the instruction of young nobles. For stories of heroes they had the epic poems like the *Mahābhārata* and the *Rāmāyaṇa*, and at a later date there were in Rājasthān many bards who wrote in verse chronicles of the deeds of heroes. These bardic chronicles begin about 700 A.D., and were composed in the vernacular.

This education was kept by the Brāhmans closely in their hands, and the various *Sūtras* and *Śāstras*, which have come down to us, written, of course, by Brāhmans, again and again insist on the duty of the Kshatriyas to protect and give honour to the Brāhmans. It was forbidden to a Kshatriya to teach,[3] and though the injunction in Manu that the king

[1] *J.R.A.S.*, 1910, pp. 966 ff. Dr. Hertel thinks between 300 B.C. and 570 A.D., and nearer the earlier limit. Dr. F. W. Thomas says at least as old as 300 A.D.

[2] Before 1400 A.D.

[3] Manu, x. 77

should learn[1] 'from the people the theory of the various trades and professions' seems to imply that in the subject of *Vārta* others besides Brāhmans might be called in to give instruction to the young princes, and this would seem probable also in the matter of military skill, yet Brāhman control dominated throughout. The king was in fact practically enjoined to regard himself as a pupil even after he had assumed his position as a ruler. Thus in Kauṭilya's *Arthaśāstra*[2] we are told—

'Him whose family and character are highly spoken of, who is well educated in the Vedas and the six Angas, is skilful in reading portents providential or accidental, is well versed in the science of government, and who is obedient, and who can prevent calamities providential or human by performing such expiatory rites as are prescribed in the *Atharvaveda*, the king shall employ as high priest. As a student his teacher, a son his father, and a servant his master, the king shall follow him. That Kshatriya breed which is brought up by Brāhmans, is charmed with the counsels of good councillors, and which faithfully follows the precepts of the *Śāstras*, becomes invincible, and attains success though unaided with weapons.'

The important position and authority thus claimed for the preceptor of the prince was no doubt influenced and intensified by the tendency in the Brāhmanic schools, which we have noticed in a previous chapter,[3] to exalt the teacher to such a position that he was regarded as an object of worship. It is quite possible that some rulers may have shaken themselves free from such a position, but the institution of the *purohita*, to whom was entrusted the religious, moral, and intellectual education of the young princes and

[1] Manu, vii. 43.
[2] *Arthaśāstra*, ch. ix. p. 17.
[3] P. 50.

nobles, continued down to very recent times. Tod, in his accounts of *Rājasthān*,[1] in referring to these *purohitas* gives rather a bad opinion of them, as men who took advantage of their position to get gain for themselves by working on the superstition of their employers. There were, no doubt, many such, who made use of their office to get wealth and honours from the king, or nobleman, who employed them. But we need not suppose that this was generally the case, and probably many of them were men of high character, whose moral influence on their pupils was distinctly good. India has had many famous rulers, who were educated under this system, and many who attained also to literary merit. Among the latter we must mention King Harsha (606 to 648 A.D.), to whom several plays and verse compositions have been ascribed.[2] As, however, in the case of the Brāhmanic education, the system of training the young Kshatriyas tended to become stereotyped, and to look too much to the authority of the past for its ideals and practice, and thus it failed to preserve its vitality as an educational force.

Among the noble warriors of India there grew up a spirit of chivalry, very much like that which prevailed in Europe in the Middle Ages. William Ward,[3] referring to a work in Sanskrit on the military arts called *Dhanur Veda*, says, 'It was contrary to the laws of war to smite a warrior overcome by another, or one who had turned his back, or who was running away; or one fearful, or he who had asked for quarter, or he who had declined further fighting, or one unarmed; or a single charioteer who had alone survived in the engagement; or one deranged; or females, children, or old men'. There were certain rules also with regard to combats. In fighting, for instance, with the club, it was

[1] Tod's *Rājasthān*, 407.

[2] V. A. Smith, *Early Hist. of India* (2nd ed.), p. 316; Macdonell's *Sanskrit Literature*, pp. 361 f.

[3] Ward, ii. 461.

unlawful to strike below the navel. Wrestling seems to have been popular in India, and still is at the present day. Many wrestling schools exist which have strict rules as to what is considered allowable. Tod[1] mentions that amongst the Rājput tribes, which were organized on a kind of feudal basis, youthful candidates were initiated to military fame in much the same way as young men in Europe in the Middle Ages became knights. The ceremony of initiation was called '*kharg bandāī*', or binding of the sword, and took place when the young Rājput was considered fit to bear arms. At this ceremony the young warrior was presented with a lance, and his sword was buckled to his side. The spirit of chivalry thus inculcated must have set before these young nobles a high ideal of valour and virtue, and this is reflected in the epic stories and in the bardic chronicles of *Rājasthān*, which contain many stories of noble deeds and knightly heroism. The typical warrior hero of India is found in Rāma, whose story is told not only in the Sanskrit *Rāmāyaṇa* of Vālmīki, but in many vernacular imitations, of which the most famous is the Hindī *Rāmāyaṇa* of Tulsī Dās (or *Rām Charit Mānas*), which was written about 1600 A.D. Indian authors never tire of telling the story of this hero again and again, and although it is possible to criticize many points in Rāma's character, it certainly holds forth a high ideal of life and virtue.

We may say that the education of the young Indian nobles was not inferior to that of the European knights in the times of chivalry, and was very much like it in many respects. The note of personal ambition and of adventure for adventure's sake seems much less prominent in the Indian ideal than in the European, and perhaps hardly existed, and the gentler virtues such as patience and filial devotion were much more emphasized, as we see in the story of Rāma. The idea that the king and the nobles had a duty to perform to society in

[1] Tod, 63, 512.

the protection of the weak, and that their position was not one so much of glory and of ease as of service to others, is very prominent. No doubt many of them failed to live up to this noble ideal, but in formulating it and holding it before the rising generation of young Kshatriyas, India has much of which to be proud.

Agricultural and Trading Classes.—As in the case of the Kshatriyas, the control of the education of the Vaiśyas, or trading and agricultural class amongst the Aryans, early came under Brāhman control. Thus we find in the earliest extant *Sūtras* [1] that the Vaiśyas, as well as the Brāhmans and Kshatriyas, were expected to receive initiation as a preliminary to entering upon the study of the Veda; and in Manu it is said,[2] 'Let the three twice-born castes, discharging their prescribed duties, study the Veda'. We have seen how in the case of the Kshatriyas the study of the Veda was attenuated, or perhaps we may say that it was developed by specialization in certain directions to meet the special needs of the young nobles and warriors. With regard to the Vaiśyas,[3] trade, rearing cattle, and agriculture were regarded as their special pursuits, and in fitting themselves for these they would have less benefit from the Vedic schools than the Kshatriyas had for their future vocation. It would seem likely that the study of the Veda became more attenuated for them than even for the Kshatriyas, and that at a quite early date the majority of them ceased to avail themselves of their privilege of attending the Brāhmanic schools, except perhaps for a very short period. In the Law of Manu[4] the functions of a Vaiśya are thus described: 'A Vaiśya must never conceive this wish, "I will not keep cattle", and if a Vaiśya is willing to keep them, they must never be kept by men of other castes. A Vaiśya must know the respective value of gems, of pearls, of corals,

[1] Gautama, i.
[2] Manu, x. 1.
[3] *Ibid.*, x. 79.
[4] *Ibid.*, ix. 328-332.

of metals, of cloth made of thread, of perfumes, and of condiments. He must be acquainted with the manner of sowing seeds, and of the good and bad qualities of fields, and he must perfectly know all measures and weights. Moreover, the excellence and defects of commodities, the advantages and disadvantages of different countries, the probable profit and loss on merchandise, and the means of properly rearing cattle. He must be acquainted with the proper wages of servants, with the various languages of men, with the manner of keeping goods, and the rules of purchase and sale'. The duties thus outlined would require that a young Vaiśya, besides a knowledge of agriculture, should also know the rudiments of commercial geography, arithmetic, and some languages, as well as the practical details of trade. With regard to these subjects it is probable that at first they were learnt by the boy from his father in the course of business, and probably amounted in most cases to little more than the minimum which would be necessary for the successful carrying on of the particular trade in which he was engaged. Thus a knowledge of 'the various languages of men' need not have meant more than a slight acquaintance with the speech of foreigners with whom trade brought him into touch, picked up in his intercourse with them, and a knowledge of 'the advantages and disadvantages of different countries' would be gathered in the same way. Thus the education of the young Vaiśya, apart from his study of the Veda, would at the earliest period, as a rule, be domestic, and he would learn from his father in the actual course of business. It is to be noted, however, that there exist in India at the present time what are called *mahājani* schools. These schools exist in several market towns where the *mahājans*, or traders, have combined to pay a teacher. They teach chiefly the special kind of writing used by the *mahājans* and arithmetic, and give sufficient education to enable a boy to help his father afterwards in trade. These schools are amongst the indigenous primary schools which will be referred to in a later chapter. They have probably existed from old times, but like so many things in India, it is difficult to say whether they are really very ancient or not. But whenever they started it must have been because the traders found it more satisfactory for a boy to have acquired some education before he began actual work in the shop. It is not impossible that the indigenous primary schools started in this way. Of this more will be said later. They are evidence that the Brāhmanic schools failed to supply the real needs of the community even in the matter of teaching reading and writing, and that other castes felt compelled to start more useful schools of their own.

Craftsmen.—As time went on the original four castes of early times became very greatly divided and subdivided. The Brāhman and Kshatriya castes still held their position, but the Vaiśyas became mingled with the masses of the surrounding population. In course of ages the number of castes became very numerous, and specially all those engaged in particular occupations became separated from others as castes. There came to be, for example, castes of carpenters, tailors, goldsmiths, and large numbers of others similar. In modern times a man does not always follow the profession or trade of his particular caste, but in ancient times probably all, or almost all, did so. The technical and professional skill developed in each caste was passed on from generation to generation.

India is a land of villages, and even at the present day with a growing commercial activity it is said that nine-tenths of the population live in villages. Each village is usually an agricultural community[1] more or less self-contained. But craftsmen are needed by the husbandman, so besides the farmers and agricultural labourers there dwell in each village

[1] See *The Indian Craftsman*, A. K. Coomaraswamy, ch. i.

certain artisans and others. In addition to the Brāhman priest and *jyotishi*, or astrologer, there may be carpenter, blacksmith, potter, and washerman. Others who are present may be the barber (who also performs some surgical operations), the scavenger, the tailor, the leather worker, the goldsmith, and so on. These craftsmen have certain privileges, and are entitled to certain payments in grain from the farmer for their services. The position of these persons and the manner of their payment varies in different parts of India, but the same features are everywhere found.

Some of the occupations are very ancient. In the *Ṛigveda Saṃhitā*[1] the following are mentioned: carpenter, physician, priest, blacksmith, poet, female grinder of corn. The construction of chariots is often alluded to, and the Ṛibhus are mentioned as celebrated workers in wood and metal. Weaving, boat-building, leather-working, agriculture, and irrigation are also referred to.

It was the villages which were the strongholds of the traditionary arts and crafts of India, but many of the craftsmen also lived in towns.[2] Here those employed in the same occupation were drawn together in trade guilds. Sometimes the craftsmen of a particular trade all belong to one caste, in which case the bonds which unite them are very strong indeed, and no outsider would be admitted. But where the same trade is pursued by men of different castes the guild may bring them together, and, though membership is hereditary, newcomers can be admitted by paying a fee, but no unqualified person is allowed to remain in the guild, or to become a member of it. There are no indentures of apprenticeship, but a boy born in one of the castes learns the particular craft from his father, and eventually takes the place

[1] Muir, *Original Sanskrit Texts*, v. 464: *Ṛigveda*, ix. 112; i. 110, 3; i. 111, 1.

[2] See *The Industrial Arts of India*, Sir Geo. Birdwood, pp. 131 ff.; Coomaraswamy, ch. ii.

of his father as a member of the guild. The guild raises funds, chiefly by fines, which are spent mostly in charities. The hours of work are regulated, and also the amount to be done, and in old times the guild also controlled the standard of quality both of material and design. The guild is also a kind of mutual assurance society. Each guild is managed by its *mahājans* (*i.e.* 'great men') or *seths*. In large cities the guilds command great influence.

The origin and age of these trade guilds is uncertain, but in the *Rāmāyaṇa* in the account of Bharata going out in procession to seek Rāma, the craftsmen are mentioned [1] as accompanying him as well as the 'foremost merchants':—

'And all others, and the foremost merchants as well as all the principal classes, joyfully went in quest of Rāma, and a number of gem-cutters, and goodly potters, weavers, and armourers, and peacock-dancers, sawers, and perforators of gems, glass-makers, and workers in ivory, cooks, incense-sellers, well-known goldsmiths, and wool manufacturers, bathers in tepid water, shampooers, physicians, makers of *dhūpas*, and wine-sellers, washermen, and tailors and actors.'

This may imply the existence of some organization of the craftsmen into guilds before the time of Vālmīki, and guilds of artisans are also referred to in Kauṭilya's *Arthaśāstra*.[2]

In modern times their influence has weakened from various causes, but they still exist, and the account of the guilds of Āhmadābād, as given in the *Imperial Gazetteer of India*,[3] is a good illustration of the system:—

'In consequence of the importance of its manufactures in silk and cotton, the system of caste or trade unions is more fully developed in Āhmadābād than in any other part of Gujarāt. Each of the different castes of traders, manufacturers,

[1] *Rāmāyaṇa* of Vālmīki, Griffith's translation, p. 417; see also Birdwood, p. 131.

[2] *Arthaśāstra*, iv. 1.

[3] *I.G.I.*, vol. v. 101.

and artisans forms its own trade guild, to which all heads of households belong. Every member has a right to vote, and decisions are passed by a majority. In cases where one industry has many distinct branches there are several guilds. Thus among potters, the makers of bricks, of tiles, and of earthen jars are for trade purposes distinct; and in the great weaving trade, those who prepare the different articles of silk and cotton form distinct associations. The object of the guilds is to regulate competition among the members, *e.g.* by prescribing days or hours during which work shall not be done. The decisions of the guilds are enforced by fines. If the offender refuses to pay, and the members of the guild all belong to one caste, the offender is put out of the caste. If the guild contains men of different castes, the guild uses its influence with other guilds to prevent the recusant member from getting work. Besides the amount received from fines, the different guilds draw an income by levying fees on any person beginning to practise his craft. This custom prevails in the cloth and other industries, but no fee is paid by potters, carpenters, and other inferior artisans. An exception is also made in the case of a son succeeding his father, when nothing has to be paid. In other cases the amount varies in proportion to the importance of the trade from Rs.50 to Rs.500. The revenue derived from these fees, and from fines, is expended in feasts to the members of the guild, and in charity. Charitable institutions or *sadā-vart*, where beggars are fed daily, are maintained in Āhmadābād at the expense of the trade guilds.'

In ancient times the arts and crafts were encouraged by kings and great nobles, and many of them kept their own craftsmen who were organized on a semi-feudal[1] basis. Sometimes they were in the service of a temple or monastery. The position of such craftsmen was secure and hereditary.

[1] Coomaraswamy, ch. iii.; Birdwood, p. 141.

Royal craftsmen are said to have been established even as early as King Aśoka. Many of the Muhammadan rulers were great patrons of the craftsmen. But the patronage of the rich was not always an unmixed blessing. Thus in mentioning the royal encouragement of the arts Bernier[1] complains that forced service was sometimes resorted to by rich patrons and also intimidation, and the Abbé Dubois[2] also in praising Indian craftsmen attributes their not having reached a higher standard of perfection to the cupidity of the rulers. If an artisan, he says, excelled in his craft he was carried off to the palace and confined there for the rest of his life, without remission of toil and little reward. Dubois believed that arts and manufactures would have made greater progress in India if the rulers had given them real encouragement.

But however this may be, one may certainly say that the spirit of fine art and of craftsmanship has existed in India for long centuries, and has still a future before it. In ancient times the caste system, with its many disadvantages, helped to keep up the standard of work, and the dexterity and skill of each particular trade was handed down from father to son.[3] Each craftsman and each caste was considered as in duty bound to perform his or its particular work for the good of society.

The system of education, then, for the lads of each particular trade was a domestic one.[4] They had practically no choice in the matter, but were, as a matter of course, brought up to the same trade as their fathers. Where the father was living and in good health he would usually train up his own son, and the young craftsman was, from the beginning, trained in the actual workshop. Thus not only was there a most

[1] *Bernier's Travels*, pp. 228–258.
[2] Dubois, i. 35.
[3] Birdwood, p. 129; Coomaraswamy, ch. v.
[4] *Ibid.*, ch. vi.; see also *Mediæval Sinhalese Art*, by same author, p. 63.

affectionate relation between teacher and pupil, but the training was free from the artificiality of the schoolroom. The boy was taught by observing and handling real things, and the father would take a great delight in passing on to his son the skill which he himself possessed. In the collection of jade at the Indian museum there is a large engraved bowl on which a family in the employ of the emperors of Delhi was engaged for three generations.[1]

It was not merely a question of actual teaching, but the boy would day by day absorb unconsciously the traditions and spirit of thepar ticular craft which he was learning.

In many arts and crafts drawings would be a necessary accomplishment. This was learnt[2] by the boy drawing first certain peculiar curves on a panel. After this came the drawing of certain traditional ornaments, and conventional figures of mythical animals and other forms. Drawing was not taught from nature.

In the majority of occupations a knowledge of reading and writing would not be required for the direct purposes of the craft, and would not be learnt. But certain Sanskrit works would in some occupations be learnt by heart.[3] These contained traditional rules relating to the particular craft, and would not only be learnt but also explained to the novice. The craftsman was thus taught to look to the past ages for the rules of his trade and even to regard it as having been revealed by the divine skill of Viśvakarman. Thus in South India there are persons generally of the goldsmith caste, who are called *vastu śāstrīs*, who know by heart the traditional rules regulating the building of houses, who must be consulted by those who wish to erect new houses as to all the necessary details prescribed by the ancient books.[4]

[1] Birdwood, p. 142.
[2] Coomaraswamy, *Mediæval Sinhalese Art*, p. 64.
[3] Coomaraswamy, ch. vi.
[4] Padfield, *Hindu at Home*, p. 3.

Though persons other than the three 'twice-born' castes were excluded from the study of the Vedas they were not shut out from participation in all religious rites, and in common with others would in various ways come to know something of the mythology and doctrines of the Hindu religion. Muhammadan craftsmen would, of course, have the same opportunity as others to send their boys to the *maktab*, held at the mosque, and here something of the Muhammadan religion was taught. The work of the craftsman was also accompanied by many religious rites, and it is not unknown for Hindu workmen on certain occasions even to worship their tools.

Thus the education of the young craftsman in India was entirely vocational, and even narrowly so. Though the religious side of the boy's education was not neglected, on the literary side it was very defective, and except for any treatises he might have to commit to memory in connection with his craft, he would have nothing but such scraps of folk-lore, mythology, and epic and other stories that might be handed down in the family, or related as the villagers gathered for gossip and discussion in the evenings, or taught by some wandering mendicant or temple priest. Yet as a vocational education it was not lacking in elements that made it really valuable. The affectionate and family relationship between teacher and pupils, the absence of artificiality in the instruction, and the opportunity and encouragement to produce really good work which the protection of the guild or caste gave—these were not without their influence in helping to build up a spirit of good craftsmanship, which was responsible for the production of really fine work.

Women.—The education of girls in India was, and still is, not unlike the education of the boys who were to be craftsmen, in that it was entirely domestic and vocational, in the sense that they were being prepared for that which was considered a woman's principal work the duties of the household.

There are not wanting evidences that women had a much higher status and more independence in early society than they came to have later. The position of the woman of the Aryan invaders of India was one of authority and honour, and marriage sometimes took place by free choice of man and maid. The customs of infant marriage and enforced widowhood were not prevalent among the Aryans of Vedic times. The authorship of some Vedic hymns [1] is ascribed to women, and in the deep discussions on philosophical truths which are related in the *Upanishads*, women are mentioned as taking part. Thus Gārgī Vāchaknavī [2] joins in the discussion, and Maitreyī,[3] wife of Yājnavalkya, was 'conversant with Brahman', and heard from her husband philosophical doctrines. It is also described what a man should do [4] if he wished 'that a learned daughter should be born to him'.

But even in the *Ṛigveda* we find signs that women were coming to be regarded as inferior beings and unequal to man in intellect.

Thus it is said,[5] 'Indra himself hath said, The mind of woman brooks not discipline, her intellect hath little weight'. And again,[6] 'With women there can be no lasting friendship; hearts of hyenas are the hearts of women'. By the time the code of Manu was drawn up her dependent position was fully established. It is there written:[7] 'By a girl, by a young woman, or even by an aged one, nothing must be done independently, even in her own house. In childhood a female must be subject to her father, in youth to her husband, when her lord is dead to her sons; a woman must never be

[1] Viz. *Ṛigveda*, viii. 80; x. 39, 40.
[2] *Bṛih. Ār. Up.*, iii. 6, 8.
[3] *Ibid.*, ii. 4; iv. 5.
[4] *Ibid.*, vi. 4, 17.
[5] *Ṛigveda*, viii. 34, 17.
[6] *Ibid.*, x. 95, 15.
[7] Manu, v. 147–149.

independent. She must not seek to separate herself from her father, husband, or sons; by leaving them she would make both her own and her husband's families contemptible.'

And again:[1] 'Day and night must women be kept in dependence by the males of their families. . . . Her father protects her in childhood, her husband protects her in youth, and her sons protect her in old age; a woman is never fit for independence.'

There are many other passages also which show the low esteem in which women were held at the time when these regulations came into being. They were excluded also from the study of the Veda. Early marriage had already become the custom, and the only education a girl received was one which fitted her to fulfil her duties in the household of her husband. 'Let the husband employ his wife in the collection and expenditure of his wealth, in keeping everything clean, in the fulfilment of religious duties, in the preparation of his food, and in looking after the household utensils.'[2] The training for this began in her own home under the supervision of her mother, and when she was married and went to live with her husband it would be continued, owing to the Indian custom of the non-separation of the family, by her mother-in-law. The injunction that she should be employed in the collection and expenditure of her husband's wealth would seem to imply some knowledge of simple accounts, but this did not probably amount to much, and it is often the custom for a woman in India to-day who can neither read nor write to look after her husband's money. Although shut out from the study of the Vedas and from performing a sacrifice, vow, or fast, apart from her husband, the performance of certain religious duties was specially enjoined for her, and in addition to receiving instruction in the rites and ceremonies in which she was expected to take

[1] Manu, ix. 2, 3. [2] *Ibid.*, ix. 11.

part a woman would become acquainted with something of the vast heap of mythological stories and folk-lore which have been handed down and accumulated in India from ancient times. This indeed would in most cases be the only literary education she would receive.

This was the state of the education of women in India for long centuries, but there were probably always some exceptions to the general rule. The education which certain Muhammadan princesses and other ladies of noble Muhammadan families received is referred to in the chapter on Muhammadan education. There were Hindu ladies also who received the same privileges, and amongst Hindu women who have taken a prominent and vigorous part in state affairs are Chānd Bībī of Āhmadnagar in the sixteenth century, Tārabāī among the Marāthas in the seventeenth, and Ahalya Bāī of Indore in the eighteenth. There have also been poetesses like Mīrā Bāī of the fifteenth century, and Bībī Ratan Kuar of the eighteenth century, both of whom wrote poems in the Hindī language.

The daughters of wealthy landholders received sometimes some education from their fathers or family priests. There were also no doubt some women who broke through the barriers which shut them out from learning, and Ward[1] mentions one Hati Vidyālankāra, a Kulīn Brāhman widow, who removed from Bengal to Benares and obtained many pupils there. Many female ascetics and mendicants also are said to know some Sanskrit and a still greater number to be conversant with the popular poems in the dialects of the country.

The dancing-girls who are often attached to temples and called *devadāsīs* (servants of the god) have in many cases been brought up from their infancy to lead immoral lives, but they have been famous in India for their wit and cleverness.

[1] Ward, ii. 503.

They receive some education to enable them to perform their work of reciting and singing poems at certain festivals. Dubois[1] says, 'These prostitutes are the only females in India who may learn to read, sing, and dance. Such accomplishments belong to them exclusively, and are, for that reason held by the rest of the sex in such abhorrence, that every virtuous woman would consider the mention of them as an affront.' The education of prostitutes is a very ancient custom in India. Thus with regard to them the *Arthaśāstra* of Kauṭilya says:[2] 'Those who teach prostitutes, female slaves and actresses, arts such as singing, playing on musical instruments like *vīnā*, pipe and drum, reading the thoughts of others, manufacture of scents and garlands, shampooing, and the art of attracting and captivating the mind of others shall be endowed with maintenance from the state.' Their sons also were to be trained as actors, and many of the prostitutes were to be trained for the work of spies. 'The wives of actors and others of similar profession who have been taught various languages and the use of signals shall, along with their relatives, be made use of in detecting the wicked and murdering or deluding foreign spies.'

Although with these few small exceptions Indian women have been shut out from any education except the training in domestic and religious duties mentioned above, they have generally had before them a high ideal of virtue and devotion, and when opportunities have been given them have shown themselves capable of great intellectual attainments. The very custom of *satī*, or self-immolation of the widow on her husband's funeral pyre, horrible and barbarous as it now seems even to Indian people themselves, was at least a sign of the great self-sacrifice and wifely devotion of which Indian women were capable.

As Rāma has become the national hero of India so his

[1] Dubois, p. 387. [2] *Arthaśāstra*, p. 156.

wife Sītā is regarded as an ideal for women to follow, and the ideal is by no means an unworthy one. When Rāma was banished to wander in the forest through the evil instigation of Kaikeyī, his step-mother, Sītā decided to accompany her husband and share all his hardships and difficulties. Thus she speaks[1]:—

'If the righteous son of Raghu wends to forests dark and drear,
Sītā steps before her husband wild and thorny paths to clear.
Like the tasted refuse water cast thy timid thoughts aside,
Take me to the pathless jungle, bid me by my lord abide.
Car and steed and gilded palace, vain are these to woman's life,
Dearer is her husband's shadow to the loved and loving wife!
For my mother often taught me and my father often spake
That her home the wedded woman doth beside her husband make,
As the shadow to the substance, to her lord is faithful wife,
And she parts not from her consort till she parts with fleeting life.

. . . . .

Years will pass in happy union,—happiest lot to woman given,—
Sītā seeks not throne or empire, nor the brighter joys of heaven.
Heaven conceals not brighter mansions in its sunny fields of pride,
Where without her lord and husband faithful Sītā would reside!
Therefore let me seek the jungle where the jungle rangers rove,
Dearer than the royal palace, where I share my husband's love,
And my heart in sweet communion shall my Rāma's wishes share,
And my wifely toil shall lighten Rāma's load of woe and care!'

And all through the long years of wandering and hardship and adventure she remained loyal and steadfast in spite of many sufferings endured.

In the *Mahābhārata* also there is a description of a true wife which we may set side by side with Sītā's lofty ideal.

'A wife is half the man, his truest friend;
A loving wife is a perpetual spring
Of virtue, pleasure, wealth; a faithful wife,
Is his best aid in seeking heavenly bliss;
A sweetly-speaking wife is a companion
In solitude, a father in advice,
A rest in passing through life's wilderness.'[2]

---

[1] *Rāmāyana*, R. C. Dutt's translation, pp. 41, 42.
[2] Monier-Williams, *Brahmanism and Hinduism*, p. 389.

It was, then, almost entirely an ideal of domestic virtue and capability that was set before the Indian girl, and though it was certainly very narrow and circumscribed it was in many ways a great and noble one. And the high degree in which the Indian woman in the past has realized the ideal which her somewhat narrow education held before her, is a promise that when her educational horizon shall have become enlarged, she will achieve still greater excellence in wider and yet more noble ideals.

CHAPTER III

BUDDHIST EDUCATION

AT the time when Gautama the Buddha lived and taught his doctrines, those philosophical ideas which were afterwards organized into the Vedānta, Yoga, and other systems recognized as permissible to those within the fold of Brāhmanism were already being discussed, though they had not assumed the final form as enshrined in the recognized *Sūtras*. The doctrine of *karma* and transmigration was generally accepted by thinking persons, and the question which earnest inquirers after truth sought to answer was how release could be obtained from the endless round of births and rebirths. Buddhism was one among many answers to the question, and it has its roots deep in Hindu philosophic thought. It differed from the recognized Brāhmanic philosophy, however, in several important details, and the teaching of Buddha was characterized by great earnestness and by a broad spirit of philanthropy. It might easily, however, have been assimilated as a part of the Brāhmanic system, as many other beliefs and practices were, but for the fact that it contained certain elements which were destined to bring it into hostility with that system. These included the non-recognition of the Vedas, and of the Brāhman hierarchy, as well as of the religious aspect of the caste system. Buddha carried on no crusade against any of these, but the opposition was implicit in his system, and in course of time the hostility worked itself out into a struggle for existence which ended in Buddhism ceasing to exist in

India as a separate faith, though several of its ideas were incorporated into Hinduism. For over fifteen hundred years, however, it was in vogue, and developed a system of education which was a rival of the Brāhmanic system, though in many ways similar to it.

One main difference between the Brāhmanic and Buddhist education was that the latter was not based on Vedic study and its teachers were not Brāhmans, unless those who had become converted to Buddhism. It was open to all comers, and not merely to the three 'twice-born' castes. All castes were equally admissible to the Buddhist community, though it seems to have been specially welcomed by the wealthy and respectable and supported by rich merchants and powerful rulers, to whose influence it owed a great deal for its advancement.

Lay adherents were recognized and duties laid down for their guidance, but it was a logical conclusion from Buddha's views of life that for rapid progress in spiritual improvement a life of retirement from the world was necessary, and this was urged upon those who wished to be earnest in their pursuit of freedom from earthly desires. A life of meditation in the solitude of a forest was considered to be the best of all, but from the first this was adopted only by the most earnest, and the majority of the monks, or *bhikkhus*, lived in companies in monasteries, or *viharas*. These *vihāras* formed a characteristic feature of Buddhism, and for many centuries they were widely spread in India.

In order to be admitted to the *sangha*, or community of *bhikkhus*, the conditions were very simple. The applicant must be free from certain diseases, and be neither a slave, a debtor, nor in the king's service. If under age he must first obtain the consent of his parents. The ceremony of admission is thus described in the *Vinaya Piṭaka*[1]:—

[1] *Mahāvagga*, i. 38.

'Let him who desires to receive ordination first cut off his hair and beard; let him put on yellow robes, adjust his upper robe so as to cover one shoulder, salute the feet of the *bhikkhus* with his head; and sit down squatting; then let him raise his joined hands, and tell him to say: "I take my refuge in the Buddha, I take my refuge in the Dhamma, I take my refuge in the Sangha".'

This first act of admission was called the *pabbajja*, and after admission the candidate became a novice. The ceremony for full admission was called the *upasampada* and was very similar. No one could receive the *pabbajja* ordination till he was eight years of age, nor the *upasampada* ordination till he was twenty. There were strict rules as to chastity, poverty, and abstinence from worldly pleasures, and also as to food and clothes. A few simple rules as to discipline were laid down, but the monk took no vow of obedience. Respect for superiors was required from the novice, and the chapter, consisting of at least ten monks, might impose penances for offences and even expel a *bhikkhu* from the order in case of serious offence. The usual mode of obtaining subsistence was for the monk to beg his food, taking with him his begging bowl and going from house to house. But from the first it was also permitted for wealthy laymen to invite monks to feed occasionally at their houses and even on certain occasions to take food to the monastery. The offences which were to be avoided by the members of the order are summed up in the *Pātimokkha*, a work which dates from the very early days of Buddhism. Twice every month this document should be publicly repeated in an assembly of monks at each monastery; and when this takes place a monk who has broken any rule is expected to confess his misdemeanour and a penance is imposed upon him according to the gravity of his offence. All the monks took part in the work of begging for food, but the manual labour in connection with the *vihāra* was performed by the novices, and the senior members of the community were expected to devote themselves to meditation and to trances, and to learning thoroughly the doctrines of the faith and spreading them abroad in the world. During part of the year the *bhikkhus* often travelled from place to place, spreading their doctrines and teaching the adherents of the Buddhist faith, but during the rainy season they settled down at a monastery. The residents of a monastery must often therefore have changed, and in becoming *bhikkhus* it was membership in the order rather than in any particular monastery that was obtained.

Each *sāmanera*, or novice, was required to choose a *bhikkhu*, who was a full member of the order, as his preceptor, or *upajjhāya* (or *āchāriya*). A pupil was called a *saddhivihārika*.[1]

'I prescribe, O *bhikkhus*, that young *bhikkhus* choose an *upajjhāya* (or preceptor). The *upajjhāya*, O *bhikkhus*, ought to consider the *saddhivihārika* (*i.e.* pupil) as a son; the *saddhivihārika* ought to consider the *upajjhāya* as a father. Thus these two united by mutual reverence, confidence, and communion of life, will progress, advance, and reach a high stage in this doctrine and discipline.'

The choosing of an *upajjhāya* is to be as follows:[2] 'Let him who is going to choose an *upajjhāya* adjust his upper robe so as to cover one shoulder, salute the feet of the intended *upajjhāya*, sit down squatting, raise his joined hands, and say, "Venerable Sir, be my *upajjhāya*"'. This was to be repeated three times, and if the *bhikkhu* who was addressed expressed his consent by word or gesture, then the choice was complete and the relationship of preceptor and pupil began.

There were strict regulations[3] for the conduct of the pupil towards the preceptor.

'Let him arise betimes; and having taken off his shoes and adjusted his upper robe so as to cover one shoulder let him give to the *upajjhāya* the teeth-cleanser, and water to rinse

[1] *Mahāvagga*, i. 25. [2] *Ibid.*, i. 25. [3] *Ibid.*

his mouth with. Then let him prepare a seat for the *upajjhāya*. If there is rice-milk, let him rinse the jug, and offer rice-milk to the *upajjhāya*. When he has drunk it, let him give water to the *upajjhāya*, take the jug, hold it down, rinse it properly without damaging it by rubbing, and put it away. When the *upajjhāya* has risen let him take away the seat. If the place is dirty let him sweep the place.' After this he was to help the preceptor to dress and get his alms-bowl ready if he wished to go out to beg. If the preceptor desired it, the pupil was to follow him as his attendant on the begging tour, keeping not too far away and not too near him. If the preceptor speaks he is not to interrupt him. After the begging is over the pupil was to get back quickly to the monastery, prepare a seat, get water for the washing of his feet, a foot-stool, and a towel. Then he must go and meet the preceptor and take his bowl and robe from him. He must fold the robe and attend to the clothes of the preceptor. If the preceptor wishes to eat the food in the alms-bowl, he must bring him water and then offer him food. After the meal the pupil must wash and dry the bowl and put it away, and also put away the robe. After the preceptor has risen the pupil must take away the seat, and put away the water for the washing of feet, the foot-stool and the towel. If the place was dirty he was to sweep it. Then he was to help the preceptor to bathe, getting for him cold or hot water, or accompanying him to the bathing-place if he wished to go there. The pupil also bathed at the same time, but had to dry and dress himself quickly so as to be ready to help the preceptor. After the bathing was completed he was to ask the preceptor for a discourse, or ask him questions. Elaborate directions are given as to the procedure to be followed by the novice in cleaning out the Vihāra—the cell, store-room, refectory, fire-room, etc. The novice must also see that there is drinkable water and food, and water for rinsing the mouth. The pupil was also to act as a check, as it were, upon the preceptor, in keeping him steadfast in the faith. If he became discontented the pupil was to try and appease him, or get some one else to do this. If indecision arose in his mind or he had become tainted with false doctrines the pupil was to try and win him back. If the preceptor was guilty of a grave offence, the pupil was to take care that the *sangha* sentenced him to discipline and also that he was rehabilitated after the penance was complete, but he was at the same time to get the *sangha* to forego, or mitigate, any severe discipline which it might wish to impose upon his preceptor. The pupil was to see that the robe of the preceptor was washed, or made, or dyed, according to need. He was not to accept presents, or give presents, or wait on any one else, or go out, without the permission of the preceptor. If the preceptor was sick he was to wait upon him and nurse him diligently.[1]

The preceptor, on the other hand, had his responsibility towards the pupil.[2]

'The *upajjhāya*, O *bhikkhus*, ought to observe a strict conduct towards his *saddhivihārika*. Let the *upajjhāya*, O *bhikkhus*, afford spiritual help and furtherance to the *saddhivihārika* by teaching, by putting questions to him, by exhortation, by instruction.' He was to see that he possessed an alms-bowl, a robe, and the other simple articles which a *bhikkhu* was allowed to possess. If the pupil was sick the preceptor was not only to nurse him, but to wait upon him and attend to him, just as the pupil was required to wait upon himself in health. He was to see that the pupil washed his robe, and show him how to make and dye it.

Only in certain prescribed cases could a pupil be turned away by his preceptor. A *bhikkhu* could not accept the office of preceptor till he had himself been a *bhikkhu* for ten years, and was learned and competent.[3]

These were the regulations for the mutual conduct of

[1] *Mahāvagga*, i. 25. [2] *Ibid.*, i. 26. [3] *Ibid.*, i. 27.

preceptor and pupil, which were drawn up at some early period before the days of King Aśoka. A Chinese visitor, I-Tsing, who was in India between 673 and 687 A.D., shows us how the system was working at the time of his visit. After referring to the directions in the *Vinaya* text quoted above, he says[1] :—

'The following is also the manner in which a pupil waits on his teacher in India. He goes to his teacher at the first watch and at the last watch of the night. First the teacher bids him sit down comfortably. Selecting some passages from the *Tripiṭaka*, he gives a lesson in a way that suits circumstances, and does not pass any fact or theory unexplained. He inspects his pupil's moral conduct, and warns him of defects and transgressions; whenever he finds his pupil faulty he makes him seek remedies and repent. The pupil rubs the teacher's body, folds his clothes, or sometimes sweeps the apartment and the yard. Then having examined water to see whether insects be in it, he gives it to the teacher. Thus, if there be anything to be done, he does all on behalf of his teacher. This is the manner in which one pays respect to one's superior. On the other hand, in case of a pupil's illness, his teacher himself nurses him, supplies all the medicine needed, and pays attention to him as if he were his child.

Thus the monastic system, which was an important feature of Buddhism, provided that every novice on his admission to the order should place himself under the supervision and guidance of a preceptor, and this state of pupillage was to last for ten years. I-Tsing says[2] that after five years from the time that the pupil masters the *Vinaya*, he was allowed to live apart from his teacher, but he must put himself under the care of some teacher wherever he went until ten years had elapsed after he was able to understand the *Vinaya*. The main ideas

[1] I-Tsing (Takakusu's trans.), p. 120.
[2] *Ibid.*, p. 119.

of this connection of teacher and pupil were taken over from the Brāhmanic education, and are in close similarity with it. From this provision for the instruction of novices arose the Buddhist educational system.

At first, no doubt, the primary idea was to provide for the proper instruction of the novice in the doctrines of the Buddhist faith, and to secure some supervision over his conduct while he was becoming habituated to the monastic life. Buddhism, indeed, exists to abolish ignorance, but it is not primarily concerned with the intellect or with the promotion of learning. The ignorance which is to be abolished is ignorance of a small number of practical doctrines, such as the necessary connection of sorrow with existence, and the need of extinguishing desire. The pursuit of secular knowledge would almost seem, from one point of view, to be contrary to the spirit and purpose of Buddhism, and yet we know that the Buddhist monastic institutions did become to some extent places of general learning. A person who is on his way to the attainment of perfect knowledge of things in themselves—that is, one who is determined to become a future Buddha—is called, according to the *Mahāyāna* form of Buddhism, a *Bodhisattva*. To reach this high estate he has to pass through certain stages, and among some of the stages which came to be recognized by Mahāyāna teaching are those in which intellectual pursuits and study are required.[1] This development of ideas, however, only took place after Buddhism had existed for a long time.

The practice of Buddhist education probably varied very much in different countries and at different times, and we have no evidence as to how soon monasteries became centres of educational importance, not only in the doctrines of Buddhism, but also in other subjects. No doubt the existence of Brāhmanic learning would form an example and incentive to the Buddhist monks to engage in study.

[1] See *Enc. Rel. and Ethics*, article on '*Bodhisattva*', pp. 739 ff.

We get a valuable picture of Buddhist education as it existed in India from the records left by certain Chinese Buddhist scholars, who visited India in the fifth and seventh centuries of our era. Their chief purpose in visiting India was to study Pāli and Sanskrit and secure copies of the sacred books of Buddhism to take back with them to their own land. Their long, toilsome, and dangerous journeys would hardly have been undertaken unless the fame of the Buddhist monasteries in India as places of learning had reached as far as China.

Fā-hien, who was in India between 399 and 414 A.D., makes frequent references to monasteries, and says that the regular business of the monks was to perform acts of meritorious virtue and to recite their *Sutras*, and sit wrapt in meditation.[1] In speaking of the monastery at Pāṭaliputra, or Patna, he says[2]:—

'By the side of the tope of Aśoka there has been made a Mahāyāna monastery, very grand and beautiful; there is also a Hīnayāna one; the two together containing six or seven hundred monks. The rules of demeanour and the scholastic arrangements in them are worthy of observation. Śāmans (monks) of the highest virtue from all quarters, and students, inquirers wishing to find out truth and the grounds of it, all resort to these monasteries.'

Fā-hien spent three years at Patna[3] learning Sanskrit and Sanskrit books, and making copies of the Buddhist sacred works. He stayed also at Tamralipti (near the mouth of the Hooghly) and at other places. In the Panjāb he found that the oral method of instruction was used, but in the more eastern regions of India writing was more freely used. Nālanda was visited by Fā-hien, but it had apparently no monks or monastery.

About two hundred years later came Hiuen Tsiang (629

[1] Fā-hien (Legge's trans.), p. 44. [2] *Ibid.*, p. 78.
[3] *Ibid.*, pp. 98 ff.

to 645 A.D.). He found Buddhism still flourishing, though a revival of Brāhmanism had taken place. The Mahāyāna form of Buddhism was spreading and the Hīnayāna form declining. He mentions monasteries at a great many places, but also speaks of some as in ruins. Some of these monasteries were very large, and often there were groups of them in one place. Thus at Hiraṇyaparvata, on the Ganges, there were ten *sangharāmas* (or monasteries) with about four thousand monks, and at Tamralipti also there were ten with a thousand monks. At Tiladaka, only twenty-one miles west of Nālanda, there was a monastery, with regard to which he says[1]:—

'This building has four halls, belvideres of three stages, high towers, connected at intervals with double gates that open inwards. It was built by the last descendant of Bimbisāra-rāja. He made much of high talent and exalted the virtuous. Learned men from different cities, and scholars from different countries, flock together in crowds, and reaching so far abide in this *sangharāma*. There are a thousand priests in it, who study the Great Vehicle.'

But the most important Buddhist centre of learning by this time was at Nālanda, which was famous far and wide for its learning. Hiuen Tsiang makes frequent reference to it as a place of learning, and describes it as follows[2]:—

'The priests, to the number of several thousands, are men of the highest ability and talent. Their distinction is very great at the present time, and there are many hundreds whose fame has rapidly spread through distant regions. Their conduct is pure and unblameable. They follow in sincerity the precepts of the moral law. The rules of this convent are severe and all the priests are bound to observe them. The countries of India respect them and follow them. The day is not sufficient for asking and answering profound questions.

[1] Hiuen Tsiang (Beal's trans.), vol. ii. 102.
[2] *Ibid.*, ii. pp. 170 ff.

From morning tili night they engage in discussion; the old and the young mutually help one another. Those who cannot discuss questions out of the *Tripiṭakā* are little esteemed and are obliged to hide themselves for shame. Learned men from different cities, on this account, who desire to acquire quickly a renown in discussion, come here in multitudes to settle their doubts, and then the streams of their wisdom spread far and wide. For this reason some persons usurp the name (of Nālanda students) and in going to and fro receive honour in consequence. If men of other quarters desire to enter and take part in discussions, the keeper of the gate proposes some hard questions; many are unable to answer, and retire. One must have studied deeply both old and new (books) before getting admission.' He goes on to say that seventy or eighty per cent. of such would-be residents of Nālanda failed to pass the test for admission. He also mentions a long list of celebrated teachers who lived at Nālanda and not only taught but composed treatises, commentaries, and other works.

Not very long after Hiuen-Tsiang's departure another Chinese scholar, I-Tsing, came to India. He was in the country from 673 to 687 A.D. His travels in India were not so extended as those of Fā-Hien and Hiuen-Tsiang, but he stayed ten years at Nālanda which was still a flourishing centre of learning. He says[1] with regard to it that the rites of the monastery were very strict and consequently the number of residents was great and exceeded three thousand. It had eight halls and three hundred apartments.[2] The lands in its possession contained more than two hundred villages. They had been bestowed upon it by kings of many generations. 'Thus,' says I-Tsing,[3] 'the prosperity of the religion continues ever owing to nothing but the fact that the *Vinaya* is being strictly carried out.' The hours of work and of worship in

[1] I-Tsing, p. 65. [2] *Ibid.*, p. 154.
[3] *Ibid.*, p. 65.

Nālanda, as well as in other monasteries, were regulated by using clepsydrae.[1]

I-Tsing gives us a most interesting idea of the study carried on at Nālanda. He says[2] that the pupil, after attending to the service of his teacher, 'reads a portion of scripture and reflects on what he has learnt. He acquires new knowledge day by day, and searches into old subjects month after month, without losing a minute'. In speaking of the method of learning he refers to Pāṇini's *Sūtras* and other grammatical works which he says[3] had to be learnt by heart. Apparently some preliminary study was often done before entering Nālanda, for he says that 'after studying grammar, etc., under instructors, they pass two or three years at Nālanda or in the country of Valabhi (Western India)'. Grammar seems to have been the foundation of all other studies and to have received great attention.

'Grammatical science,' he says,[4] 'is called in Sanskrit Śabdavidyā, one of the five Vidyās. (The five Vidyās are: (1) Śabdavidyā, grammar and lexicography; (2) Śilpasthānavidyā, arts; (3) Chikitsavidyā, medicine; (4) Hetuvidyā, logic; and (5) Adhyātmavidyā, science of the universal soul, or philosophy.) 'Śabda means "sound," and vidyā "science." The name for the general secular literature of India is Vyākaraṇa (*i.e.* Grammar), of which there are about five works, similar to the Five Classics of the Divine Land (China).' These five he enumerates as follows:—

(1) 'The *Siddha*—composition for beginners. . . . Children learn this book when they are six years old, and finish it in six months.'

(2) 'The *Sūtra* is the foundation of all grammatical science. . . . It contains a thousand ślokas and is the work of Pāṇini. . . . Children begin to learn the *Sūtra* when they are eight years old, and can repeat it in eight months' time.'

[1] I-Tsing, p. 145.
[2] *Ibid.*, p. 116.
[3] *Ibid.*, p. 167.
[4] *Ibid.*, pp. 169 ff.

(3) 'The book on Dhātu' (Verbal roots).

(4) 'The book on the three Khilas (or "pieces of waste land"), viz. Ashṭadhātu, Manda, and Uṇādi.' (The first deals with cases and conjugations, and the others with the formation of words from root and suffix or suffixes.) 'Boys begin to learn the book on the three Khilas when they are ten years old, and understand them thoroughly after three years' diligent study.'

(5) 'The *Vṛitti-Sūtra*' (Kāśikāvṛitti). 'This is a commentary on the foregoing *Sūtra* (*i.e.* Pāṇini's *Sūtra*). . . . Boys of fifteen begin to study this commentary, and understand it after five years.'

There thus seems to have been a long course of grammatical study of the Sanskrit language, beginning when a boy was six years of age and lasting till he was twenty, which was a preliminary to the study of higher subjects. With regard to this further study I-Tsing says[1]: 'After having studied this commentary, students begin to learn composition in prose and verse and devote themselves to logic (*hetuvidyā*) and metaphysic (*abhidharmakośa*). In learning the *Nyāyā-dvāra-tarka-śāstra* (introduction to logic), they rightly draw inferences (*anumāna*); and by studying the *Jātakamālā* (stories of Buddha in previous births) their powers of comprehension increase. Thus instructed by their teachers, and instructing others, they pass two or three years, generally in the Nālanda monastery in Central India, or in the country of Valabha (Walā) in Western India. These two places are like Chinma, Shihch'u, Lungmen, and Ch'ueli in China, and there eminent and accomplished men assemble in crowds, discuss possible and impossible doctrines, and after having been assured of the excellence of their opinions by wise men, become far-famed for their wisdom. To try the sharpness of their wit they proceed to the king's court to lay down before it the sharp weapon of their abilities; there they present their schemes and show their (political)

[1] I-Tsing, pp. 176 ff.

talent, seeking to be appointed in the practical government. When they are present in the House of Debate, they raise their seat and seek to prove their wonderful cleverness. When they are refuting heretical doctrines all their opponents become tongue-tied and acknowledge themselves undone. Then the sound of their fame makes the five mountains (of India) vibrate, and their renown flows, as it were, over the four borders. They receive grants of land and are advanced to a high rank; their famous names are, as a reward, written in white on their lofty gates. After this they can follow whatever occupation they like.'

It is apparently in connection with this higher course that he mentions certain other books which were studied, namely—

(6) 'The *Chūrṇi*' (*i.e.* the Mahābhāshya, or Great Commentary of Patanjali on Pāṇini's *Sūtras*).

(7) 'The *Bhartṛihari śāstra* treats of principles of human life as well as of grammatical science.'

(8) 'The *Vākya* discourse'—a treatise on the Inference supported by the authority of the sacred teaching, and on Inductive argument.

(9) 'The *Pei-na*' (perhaps Beda or Veda), which was a work on philosophy.

The priests also, he tells us, learned besides, all the *Vinaya* works, and investigated the *Sūtras* and *Śāstras* as well.

This valuable picture of Buddhist learning and education in the monasteries at the time of I-Tsing's visit shows a great amount of intellectual activity going on. The main course seems to have been founded on an elaborate study of Sanskrit grammar which led on to logic and finally to metaphysics and philosophy. It is closely connected with Brāhmanic education in that the first six out of the nine works which he mentions as being studied were those also used in the Brāhman schools. The last three, however, were composed, I-Tsing tells us, by Bhartṛihari,[1] who was a member of the Buddhist order. The method seems to have been chiefly oral, and he frequently insists that these various treatises must be learned by heart. I-Tsing has a passage in which he says,[2] 'There are two traditional ways in India of attaining to intellectual power: (1) Committing to memory; (2) the alphabet fixes one's ideas. By this way, after a practice of ten days or a month, a student feels his thought rise like a fountain, and can commit to memory whatever he has once heard. This is far from being a myth, for I myself have met such men.' The meaning of this passage is by no means clear, but it certainly brings out the prevalent practice of learning everything by heart and shows what facility students seem to have gained in doing this. A great place was also given to discussion and debate, at least in the higher part of the course, and a man's ability seems to have been very largely judged by his power to vanquish opponents in discussion. It was such men apparently who got royal appointments and whose names were, 'as a reward, written in white on their lofty gates.'

The *Jātaka* stories and the *Vinaya* and other texts which were studied gave some of the elements of the study of literature, and I-Tsing mentions[3] the composition of poems as one of the occupations of the residents at the monasteries. Great attention seems to have been given at Nālanda to the practice of singing or chanting, and I-Tsing was anxious that this should be introduced in his own country.

Medicine seems to have been studied, though not forming part of the ordinary course. It was no doubt taken up by specialists. I-Tsing refers to a Śāstra on medical science and makes considerable mention of various forms of medical

[1] For Bhartṛihari, see Macdonell, *Sans. Lit.*, pp. 340, 381, 382. He died in 651 A.D.

[2] I-Tsing, p. 183.

[3] *Ibid.*, p. 154.

treatment; and Fā-hien, who was in India two hundred years before I-Tsing, mentions the dispensaries and hospitals which existed at Patna.[1] Medicine seems to have been specially cultivated by the Buddhists; and Charaka, who is one of the chief Indian authorities on medicine, is said to have been the court physician of the Buddhist King Kanishka in the first century A.D. There is no evidence that law, mathematics, and astronomy were cultivated in the Buddhist schools of learning. Probably law was already regarded too much as an exclusive possession of the Brāhmans to make intrusion by others possible, while Buddhism would not have the need of astronomy that Brāhmanism had for ascertaining auspicious times for sacrifices and other ceremonial.

Though Buddhism encouraged a life of separation from the world and the suppression of desire, it did not, like Brāhmanism, advocate asceticism and bodily mortification, and the care of the bodily health was considered as of importance for improvement in the spiritual condition. We find that exercise was encouraged in the Buddhist monasteries of India, and I-Tsing tell us[2] that 'in India both priests and laymen are generally in the habit of taking walks, going backwards and forwards along a path, at suitable hours, and at their pleasure; they avoid noisy places. Firstly it cures disease, and secondly it helps to digest food. The walking hours are in the forenoon, and late in the afternoon. They either go away (for a walk) from their monasteries, or stroll quietly along the corridors. . . . If any one adopts this habit of walking he will keep his body well, and thereby improve his religious merit.'

I-Tsing seems to have had a very favourable impression of the school of learning at Nālanda where he spent so many years. He mentions by name many distinguished teachers whom he met and with whom he conversed, and says[3]: 'I

[1] Fā-hien, p. 79. [2] I-Tsing, p. 114.
[3] *Ibid.*, pp. 184, 185.

have always been very glad that I had the opportunity of acquiring knowledge from them personally, which I should otherwise never have possessed, and that I could refresh my memory of past study by comparing old notes with new ones.'

Thus arising out of the duty of the *bhikkhus* to teach and spread their doctrines and of the relation of teacher and pupil which the discipline of the order required, the Buddhist monastery had become a place where not only the Buddhist doctrines were studied, but also much secular knowledge. No doubt the content of this was meagre judged by modern standards, but it does not compare very unfavourably with the content of other ancient systems of education. Was this system of general culture confined to those who had entered the sacred order either as monks or as novices, or was it also shared by those who were preparing to take a more active part in the affairs of the world? It seems clear from what I-Tsing tells us, that the monastery was a place of instruction not only for those who had joined the order as a lifelong profession, but for others also. He tells us, for instance, in a passage quoted above, that the debate which was held in the king's court was in order that students might show their talent, and thus obtain appointments in the practical government. He also tells us that after completing their course students could 'follow whatever occupation they like.' But there is a passage which puts the matter still more clearly and leaves no doubt upon the question.[1] 'Those white-robed (laymen) who come to the residence of a priest, and read chiefly Buddhist scriptures with the intention that they may one day become tonsured and black-robed, are called "children' (*mānava*). Those who (coming to a priest) want to learn secular literature only without having any intention of quitting the world, are called "students" (*brahmachārī*). These two groups of

[1] I-Tsing, p. 105.

persons, though residing in a monastery, have to subsist at their own expense. In the monasteries in India there are many "students" who are entrusted to the *bhikkhus* and instructed by them in secular literature. On the one hand the "students" serve under priests as pages, on the other the instruction will lead to pious aspirations. It is therefore very good to keep them, inasmuch as both sides are benefited in this way.'

This passage makes it quite clear that there were in the monastery not only the professed monks and novices, but also those who were studying the Buddhist scriptures with a view to joining the order and also those who had no intention of dcing so, but were residing at the monastery only for the sake of education. This practice also may have been influenced by the Brāhman schools which were open not only to young Brāhmans who were destined for the priestly office, but to others of the twice-born castes as well. There was nothing to prevent a man who had joined the Buddhist order from returning to the world, and probably many did so, and with regard to Bhartṛihari, who composed some of the works I-Tsing refers to, he tells us [1] that he became seven times a priest, but seven times returned to the laity, and that he wrote the following verses full of self-reproval :—

> 'Through the enticement of the world I returned to the laity.
> Being free from secular pleasures again I wear the priestly cloak.
> How do these two impulses
> Play with me as if a child?'

I-Tsing adds, At last he returned to the position of a lay devotee (*upāsaka*), and wearing a white garment continued to exalt and promote the true religion, being still in the monastery.'

The story of this man illustrates what was probably frequently the case that some joined the order without

[1] I-Tsing, p. 179.

continuing in it, but it is also interesting as showing how one of the foremost teachers of the monastery was a man who did not continue in the order but finished his career as a layman.

After the visits of these Chinese pilgrims we have but scanty evidence as to the course and development of Buddhist education in India, but the monasteries long continued as centres of education and literary study, and only decayed as Buddhism itself decayed in India. Dr. S. C. Vidyabhusana [1] mentions the following mediæval centres of Buddhist learning, namely, Kānchīpura,[2] Nālanda, Odantapurī,[3] Śrī Dhanyakataka, Kāśmīra, and Vikramaśilā.

Nālanda has already been referred to above in connection with the visits of the Chinese scholars. Its site has been identified with the modern Baragaon, seven miles north of Rajgir, in Bihar. Nāgārjuna, about 300 A.D., and Ārya Deva, about 320 A.D., are said to have been the earliest scholars to take interest in Nālanda as an educational institution, but it was not till about 450 A.D. that it assumed the character of a university when it came under the recognition of the king of Magadha. It must have been at the height of its prosperity about the time of the visits[4] of Hiuen-Tsiang and I-Tsing in the seventh century A.D. The latest limit of the existence of Nālanda as a university centre which is known with certainty is 750 A.D., when a certain Kamalśīla was teaching the Tantric philosophy there. But it probably existed until about 850 A.D., for it is known that there was for some time intercourse between Nālanda and the later university of Vikramaśilā, which was not founded till about 800 A.D. 'According to Tibetan accounts the quarter in which the Nālanda University, with its grand library, was located, was called Dharmaganja ("Piety Mart"). It consisted of three grand buildings called Ratnasāgara, Ratnodadhi, and

[1] *Mediæval School of Indian Logic.*
[2] *I.e.* Conjeeveram.
[3] Or Uddandapura.
[4] See pp. 96 ff.

Ratnaranjaka. In Ratnodadhi, which was nine-storied, there were the sacred scripts called *Prajnāpāramitā-sūtra*, and Tāntric works such as *Samāja-guhya*, etc. After the Turuska raiders had made incursions in Nālanda, the temples and *chaityas* there were repaired by a sage named Mudita Bhadra. Soon after this, Kukutasiddha, minister of the king of Magadha, erected a temple at Nālanda, and while a religious sermon was being delivered there, two very indigent Tīrthika mendicants appeared. Some naughty young novice-monks, in disdain, threw washing-water on them. This made them very angry. After propitiating the sun for twelve years, they performed a *yajna*, fire sacrifice, and threw living embers and ashes from the sacrificial pit into the Buddhist temples, etc. This produced a great conflagration which consumed Ratnodadhi. It is, however, said that many of the Buddhist scriptures were saved by water which leaked through the sacred volumes of *Prajnāpāramitā-sūtra* and *Tantra*.'[1]

From the foregoing account it will be seen that in the later years at least of Nālanda the Tantric form of Buddhism was studied there, that is, a variety of Mahāyāna Buddhist doctrine, which was closely allied to the Hindu cult of Śiva and illustrates the gradual assimilation of Indian Buddhism to Hinduism. Two other centres of learning which came into being as Nālanda declined were both strongholds of Tantric Buddhism. These were Odantapuri and Vikramaśilā.

The monastery of Odantapuri, or Uddandapura, was founded by a certain Gopāla, who was king of Bengal and extended his power westwards over Magadha, or South Bihar. It dates from about the middle of the eighth century A.D.[2]

Vikramaśilā[3] had a monastery which is said to have included 107 temples and six colleges. It was founded by

[1] *Mediæval School of Indian Logic*, Appendix A.

[2] V. A. Smith, *Hist. of India*, 3rd edition, p. 397.

[3] *Mediæval School of Indian Logic*, Appendix C.

King Dharmapāla at the close of the eighth century A.D. It was situated in Bihar on a hill on the right bank of the Ganges, but its precise position is not certain. King Dharmapāla endowed his foundation with rich grants which were to be used for the maintenance of 108 resident monks as well as non-resident monks and pilgrims. A learned and pious sage was always appointed as the head of the monastery. Among the subjects studied were grammar, metaphysics (including logic), and ritualistic books. Pandits who were eminent for learning and character were rewarded by having their images painted on the walls of the university, and the title of 'pandit' was conferred on distinguished scholars by the king himself. Six of the most learned of the sages of this foundation were appointed to guard its gates. This university was destroyed by the Muhammadan invader Bakhtiyar Khiljī about 1203 A.D.

It seems that, apart from the monasteries, Buddhism did not offer any educational opportunities, but we have to ask the question as to how far, during all the centuries that Buddhism existed in India, Buddhist education influenced the general mass of the people, at least those who adhered to Buddhism, and provided opportunities of popular instruction. In more modern times in some Buddhist countries it is said that almost all boys went to the monastery and received at least some elementary education at the hands of the monks. Thus in Burma, before the country came under British control, almost the whole male population passed through the monasteries, and were taught by the monks.[1] Those who did not intend to join the religious order stayed till they were about twelve years of age, and received instruction in reading, writing, and arithmetic, as well as some religious instruction. There is no doubt that this system of popular education in connection with the Buddhist monastery is an ancient custom,

[1] Shway Yeo, ch. ii.

and it has been claimed that the presence of Buddhist monasteries in India in ancient times implies a widespread, popular education there during the time that they flourished.[1] There does not, however, seem to be any very clear evidence of this, and we cannot say how soon it became the practice for the monasteries to give education of a popular kind. The question of the origin of popular education in India will be discussed in the later chapter on that subject, but it may be said here, that even if facilities existed for general instruction as early as the reign of King Aśoka, it was not necessarily in connection with the monasteries that it was given.

At the time of the visit of Fā-hien, however (399–414 A.D.), we find that the monasteries seem to have begun to undertake instruction of a more general kind than merely instructing those who joined the *sangha* in the precepts of Buddhism. In speaking of the monasteries at Patna, he says[2] that the rules of demeanour and the scholastic arrangements in them were worthy of observation, and that students and inquirers wishing to find out the truth and the grounds of it resorted thither. In a note on Fā-hien's reference to the 'scholastic arrangements' at Patna, Prof. Legge says: 'Why should there not have been schools in those monasteries in India as there were in China? Fā-hien himself grew up with other boys in a monastery, and no doubt had to go to school. And the next sentence shows us there might be schools for more advanced students as well as for the *srāmaneras*.' There seems no reason to doubt that by the time of Fā-hien the monasteries may have given some general instruction not only to young novices, but even to pupils who had no intention of joining the *sangha*. At all events this system was in full swing at the time of I-Tsing's visit. But even the presence of pupils who were not intending to join the order of monks does not warrant us, without other evidence, in thinking that such education was

[1] V. A. Smith, *Aśoka*, p. 108.

[2] Fā-hien, p. 78.

taken advantage of by a large proportion of the children of Buddhist parents, or included popular elementary instruction. The education which I-Tsing describes was education of a higher rather than of a popular type, and was based on a profound and lengthy study of Sanskrit grammar. It would, of course, seem likely that there were arrangements for teaching reading and writing to the lads who were taking this course, but I-Tsing makes no mention of this, nor of the teaching of arithmetic. It is not, therefore, possible to say for certain, even at the time of I-Tsing's visit, whether literacy was widely diffused amongst the Buddhist population or not. It would seem, however, not unlikely that when once the monasteries had begun to receive pupils who were not intending to join the community the system might have been gradually extended, and to have catered even for boys who only came to learn the three R's and receive some simple religious instruction, and the analogy of Buddhist schools as they exist in Burma and Ceylon even down to the present day would seem to confirm this. If, as seems not unreasonable to suppose, the Buddhist monasteries came to supply a good deal of popular elementary instruction, the decay of Buddhism and the consequent disappearance of the monasteries would have meant that this method of giving popular education would also have gradually come to an end, and so the need would arise for this education to be supplied in some other way. This may have been one amongst other causes which led to the spread of the indigenous elementary schools in India.

A description of the education carried on in Ceylon in a Buddhist school, as given by a writer[1] who wrote about the middle of last century, may help us to form some picture of what the Buddhist schools in India were probably like, though difference of country and lapse of time may have brought many changes. He says that there was generally a school

[1] R. S. Hardy, *Eastern Monachism*, pp. 18 and 313 ff.

attached to a *pansal*, or residence of a Buddhist priest. The children did not all attend at the same period of day, but as they had leisure went to the *pansal* to repeat their lessons, and then returned home, or went to their employment in some other place. The school was a mere shed open at the sides, with a raised platform in one corner covered with sand, on which letters were traced by the finger of the child learning to write. Lessons were usually repeated aloud, and were recited in a singing tone, several boys frequently joining in chorus. The alphabet was first learned, and was usually copied upon *tal* leaves; after that the union of vowels and consonants. Then the pupil began to write the letters upon sand, holding in the left hand a piece of wood to erase what he had written. The course of reading included about fourteen books: (1) A name book, which was a collection of names of villages, countries, temples, caves, etc.; (2) an enumeration of the various signs and beauties upon the person of Buddha; (3) stanzas in honour of Buddha, Truth, etc., with some grammatical rules also; (4) an account of the birth of Ganeśa, etc.; (5) stanzas in praise of Buddha in Elu, Pāli, and Sanskrit; (6) Navaratna ('The Nine Jewels')—a description and eulogy of nine most precious things in the world, the principal of which is Buddha; (7) Sanskrit proverbs with explanations; (8) Sanskrit stanzas in honour of Buddha with explanation; (9) Sanskrit stanzas containing the names of the last twenty-four Buddhas, etc.; (10) Pāli stanzas in honour of Buddha; (11) Sanskrit stanzas in honour of the sun; (12) Sanskrit stanzas on the management of the voice in recitation; (13) Pāli stanzas in honour of Buddha; (14) the Amarakośa, or Sanskrit lexicon, with a Singhalese commentary. This was the complete curriculum for a Singhalese student unless he was preparing for the priesthood or for the medical profession. Even this course was only completed by a few of the boys who attended the *pansal* schools.

In schools in Buddhist monasteries in Burma [1] the condition of affairs is very similar,[2] or, at least, was so before the introduction of Western ideas of education. When a boy is about eight or nine years of age he goes as a pupil to the monastery, which is open to all, rich and poor alike. He does not, however, become a novice until twelve or fifteen years of age, when it is the custom to assume the yellow robe of the monastic order at least for a short time. Some boys are boarders, others attend the monastery every day. The instruction begins by teaching a boy the letters of the alphabet written on a rough wooden slate. These he learns by shouting them out at the top of his voice. All the books which are learnt are religious ones, and the curriculum includes the learning of Pāli formulæ and prayers necessary for religious worship. The life and sayings of Buddha and the Jātakas are the chief elements of instruction. The pupils repeat their lessons word for word after their teacher, as they sit in rows before him, and chant after him all in the same key. The amount of secular learning, arithmetic, and so on, is of the most meagre possible description. Boys designated for a monastic life stay on permanently, but those intended for lay life leave at twelve years of age or even earlier. Nowadays many boys attend the government or mission schools, but they often go to the monastery first. Although the curriculum in the monastic schools is of such a meagre description, the educational opportunities which they have provided have led to a very high percentage of literacy amongst the male population of Burma, which is very much higher than in any province of British India.

The Buddhist monastic order includes not only monks but

[1] For an interesting account of Buddhist education as it exists in Tibet to-day, see *Indian Pandits in the Land of Snow*, by S. C. Das, 1893, pp. 3–11.

[2] Shway Yeo, ch. ii.

also nuns (*bhikkhunis*). It was only with great reluctance that the Buddha consented to this arrangement. His aunt, Mahāprājāpati, wished to join the order, but was refused three times. She appealed to Ānanda, who interceded for her, and at last the Buddha yielded. He expressed, however, his sorrow, and said that the admission of women would ruin his work. If they had not been admitted, the doctrine, he said, would have abided a thousand years, but now it would only abide five hundred. The nuns were made closely dependent on the monks, and could only be admitted by them; and there are passages which show that the Buddha shared the low opinion of women which was held by others in India, as we see expressed, for instance, in the Law of Manu. We have no means of ascertaining to what extent Buddhist nunneries spread, and what proportion in numbers they bore to the monasteries. It would seem most likely that they would be much fewer in number, and this is borne out by what is found in Buddhist countries to-day. In Ceylon Buddhist nuns are hardly to be found, and in Burma they are small in numbers compared with the monks. It is not likely, therefore, that Buddhist nunneries in India helped to any great extent to spread education amongst women. No doubt those who joined the order would have received instruction in the Buddhist doctrines, and perhaps also in reading and writing; but we do not know whether the nunneries, like the monasteries, became centres of general instruction, receiving pupils even from amongst those who were not intending to join the order. There is no evidence of this, and the probability seems rather against our supposing it was so. In Ceylon there are no such nunneries to-day where girls are instructed, and in Burma little is done for the education of girls compared with what is done for boys. Some Buddhist nuns visit, it is said, the women in their homes, and there are a few girls' schools at the nunneries, but that is all. It seems hardly safe, therefore, to conjecture that even when Buddhism was at its zenith in India it did very much for the education of women.

Apart from the monasteries or nunneries Buddhism did not provide educational opportunities, but the sons of Buddhist laymen, who did not go to the *sangharāma* for instruction, would learn their own craft or profession from their fathers in the same way as other Indian craftsmen, and had also the opportunity of attending whatever popular schools may have existed.

Buddhism has passed away from India, but has left a considerable influence upon Indian philosophic thought and religious ideals; but on the educational side it is difficult to estimate the amount of its influence. Its curriculum was meagre, and, such as it was, was mostly borrowed or adapted from the Brāhmanic schools. The Vedas were replaced by its own sacred books. Medicine and logic[1] seem to have been the two subjects in which the Buddhist schools were distinguished, if we leave out of account their influence on philosophic thought. Mediæval Indian logic from about 400 to 1200 A.D. was almost entirely in the hands of Jains and Buddhists, and their books on this subject are very numerous. The Buddhist educational ideals and practice also were derived from, or closely connected with, those of Brāhmanism. It is not, however, improbable that in breaking down the monopoly of the Brāhmanic schools and offering the possibility of education to men of all castes, Buddhism may have done something to extend amongst the people of India the desire for some popular education besides the training of the young craftsmen, and to have stimulated a demand which led to the growth of the popular elementary schools which are described in a later chapter.

[1] For Buddhist logic, see *The Mediæval School of Indian Logic*, by Dr. S. C. Vidyabhusana.

CHAPTER IV

MUHAMMADAN EDUCATION

THE Muhammadans first appeared in India in the eighth century A.D., but the real storm of Muhammadan aggression burst on India under Mahmūd of Ghaznī, who is said to have made no less than seventeen raids into India from 1000 to 1026 A.D. He was a stern opponent of idolatry, and with fierce iconoclastic zeal he broke down temples and smashed idols and carried off many captives and much wealth to his own capital. To the inhabitants of India Mahmūd must have appeared as anything but a promoter of education and learning, for during his raids the Brāhman educational centres often suffered severely, and the learned Brāhmans, who lived and taught there, were often killed or put to flight. In his own kingdom of Ghaznī, Mahmūd,[1] however, was a great patron of education on Muhammadan lines. He gave large sums of money for the support of learned men and poets, and at his capital he established a seat of learning which was resorted to by literary men from far and near. Amongst them was the poet Firdausī. Mahmūd's immediate successor is said to have founded schools and colleges, and the patronage of learning was continued. All this, however, was really outside India.

The permanent settlement of Muhammadans in India, and the conversion, whether by force or persuasion, of some of the inhabitants to Islām meant the establishment of mosques, and

[1] N. N. Law, *Promotion of Learning in India by Muhammadans*, pp. 3 ff.; Ferishta (trans. by J. Briggs), i. 61.

as in other Muhammadan countries, the mosque, especially in towns, was a centre of instruction and of literary activity. Muhammadan educational institutions are distinguished as *maktabs* or *madrasahs*. The *maktab* is a primary school attached to a mosque, the chief business of which is to instruct boys in those portions of the Korān which a Muhammadan is expected to know by heart in order to perform his devotions and other religious functions. Sometimes instruction in reading, writing, and simple arithmetic is also included in the curriculum. The *madrasah* is a school or college of higher learning.

Mahmūd's successors were unable to hold what their father had won, and a new power arose at Ghor, west of Ghaznī, which overthrew the Ghaznawids. It was Muhammad Ghorī (1174–1206) who really laid the foundations of the Muhammadan domination of India. In 1192 he established his power at Delhi. Muhammad Ghorī is reported to have destroyed some temples at Ajmere, and to have built in their places mosques and colleges.[1] He had a great fancy for adopting some of his promising young slaves and giving them a good education. This education combined training in the work of governing with literary instruction. Amongst the slaves whom he thus educated was Kutb-ud-dīn, who succeeded his master in 1210 at Delhi, and was the first of what is called the Slave Dynasty. Kutb-ud-dīn was a man of literary tastes, and although, like many other Muhammadan rulers, he destroyed Hindu temples, he built many mosques which were centres not only of religious worship but also of education. An officer of his, named Bakhtiyār, destroyed at Vikramaśilā in Bihār a Buddhist monastic institution which was a place of learning, but he also is said to have been an establisher of mosques and colleges.[2] There is mention [3] of a *madrasah*, or college, built

[1] Law, pp. 17, 18.
[2] *Ibid.*, pp. 19, 20; Ferishta, i. 190.
[3] Law, p. 21.

by Altamsh (1210–1236), the successor of Kutb-ud-dīn; and his daughter Razīya, who ruled after her father's death, was a woman of some education, and was a patron of learning. A college existed at Delhi during her reign.[1] Nasīr-ud-dīn (1246–1266) and Balban (1266–1287) both encouraged learning.[2] The former is said to have been a student, and in Balban's reign many literary societies are said to have flourished at Delhi under the patronage of his son, Prince Muhammad.[3] There is mention of a college at Jalandhar in the reign of Nasīr-ud-dīn. Balban's successor was a profligate youth who gave no encouragement to men of letters.

In the Khaljī dynasty (1290–1320) Jalāl-ud-dīn was a man of great literary tastes, but not so Alā-ud-dīn, who not only showed no favour to learned men but confiscated the endowments which had been given for their support by his predecessors. By this time, however, Delhi had become a great centre of learning, and continued to be so in spite of the discouraging policy of Alā-ud-dīn. The endowments were restored by his successor, who was in other ways a worthless character.

Under the Tughlak monarchs[5] (1325–1413) Muhammadan education in India seems to have made considerable progress. It was encouraged by Ghiyās-ud-dīn Tughlak; and his successor, Muhammad Tughlak, is said to have been a man of great learning who gave great encouragement and help to scholars. But his good intentions and efforts were to a great extent spoiled by the wild scheme he projected of building a capital at Daulatābād and compelling all the inhabitants of Delhi to migrate to the new city. This caused great misery, which was hardly alleviated by the citizens being allowed to return to their old homes when the scheme fell through. This was a great set-back to Delhi as a centre of education

[1] Law, p. 22. [2] *Ibid.*, p. 25. [3] *Ibid.*, p. 24.
[4] *Ibid.*, pp. 30–41. [5] *Ibid.*, pp. 42 ff.

and learning, as it became bereft of its scholars. It was some time before it could recover. Fīrūz Tughlak was more successful in his attempt to found a new Delhi, which he called Fīrūzābād. This city became famous as a literary centre, and Fīrūz, who was himself an educated man, gave great encouragement to scholars, and bestowed gifts and pensions upon them.[1] Like some of the Muhammadan sovereigns of India before him he had a special interest in educating young slaves, though he carried it to a further extent than any of his predecessors. It is said that he maintained no fewer than eighteen thousand of these lads, and large sums must have been spent by him for their support and education. He had some of them apprenticed to craftsmen, while others were set to learn the Korān or the art of copying manuscripts. In the inscription which Fīrūz placed upon a mosque in his capital of Fīrūzābād, he mentions[2] amongst his other good works the repair of schools and the alienation of revenue for their support. The Muhammadan historian Ferishta says[3] that Fīrūz built no less than thirty colleges with mosques attached. In the college which he founded at his capital students and professors all lived together in the institution, and stipends and scholarships were given for their support. It is evident that under this sovereign considerable advance must have been made in the education of Muhammadans. The invasion of Taimūr (1398), with its horrors of bloodshed and rapine, must have been as great a set-back to education as it was to the political power of the Delhi kingdom. In the time of Sayyid Alā-ud-dīn, Badaun became a great centre of learning,[4] and under Sikandar Lodī, Agra, which had been made the capital by his predecessor, also came into prominence as a literary centre.[5] Sikandar insisted on all his military officers having a literary education.

[1] Ferishta, i. 462. [2] *Ibid.*, i. 464, 465. [3] *Ibid.*, i. 464, 465.
[4] Law, p. 71. [5] *Ibid.*, p. 73.

The *madrasahs* and *maktabs* were confined to Muhammadans, but by this time Hindus and Muhammadans had begun to study one another's languages. The sacred language of Islām was, of course, Arabic, but Persian was the court language of the Muhammadan conquerors of India, and a knowledge of Persian, and perhaps sometimes also of Arabic, would be necessary for Hindus who held important offices under government. The appointment of Hindus to such offices was beginning to take place. Fīrūz Shāh, for instance, gave to two Hindus very responsible posts in his administration.[1] The Muhammadans also were beginning to translate Hindu books into Persian, which involved a knowledge of the Hindu languages. In the reign of Sikandar Lodī the movement developed greatly,[2] and it was about that time that the study of Persian by Hindus began in earnest. The intercourse between the Muhammadans and Hindus led to the formation of a new language which came to be called Urdu.[3] It is an application of Western Hindi to the common purposes of all classes. It is generally written in Persian characters and has many words of Arabic and Persian origin. The word *Urdu* means literally 'camp', but the Mughals of India used it only with regard to the Imperial Camp.[4] Urdu was thus the 'camp language' in that sense.

While the paramount sovereigns at Delhi were thus developing education amongst their Muhammadan subjects, many of the monarchs of the lesser Muhammadan states, which had become independent of Delhi during the period of disorder which had followed the death of Fīrūz Shah, were also showing great activity in this direction. In the Bahmanī kingdom of the Deccan there is the record of the founding of

[1] Law, p. 64. [2] *Ibid.*, p. 75.

[3] *Calcutta Rev.*, 1884, art. 'Mediæval India', by H. G. Keene, pp. 74, 75.

[4] Keene, *Moghul Empire*, p. 6.

several colleges and schools.[1] The college which Mahmūd Gāwān, minister of Muhammad Shāh (1463–1482), built at Bīdar, is said to have possessed a library of three thousand volumes. Some of the Bahmanī sovereigns made provision for the education of orphans, appointing funds for their support, and for the learned men engaged to teach them. It has been said that this kingdom possessed a high standard of education according to the current Muhammadan ideas, and that there were many village schools. Education was also encouraged and colleges built in the states of Bījāpur, Golkonda, Mālwā, Khāndesh, Jaunpur, Mūltān, and Bengal.[2] The Chahār Minār, which still exists in Haidarābād (Golkonda), once contained a college. In the state of Jaunpur, the capital city of the same name was one of the most famous seats of Muhammadan learning in India in the Middle Ages. It came into prominence during the reign of Ibrāhīm Sharki (1402–1440), and although Sikandar Lodī destroyed its colleges when he conquered Jaunpur, it regained its position as an educational centre. Scholars from far and near came to study here, and amongst the students was one at least, Sher Shāh,[3] who afterwards became the paramount Muhammadan sovereign of India. Having quarrelled with his father, who was ruling in Bengal, he went to Jaunpur, and when his father wrote demanding his return, he replied that Jaunpur was a better place of education than Sasarām. The subjects which he studied were history, poetry, and philosophy, and he learnt by heart the Persian poems of Sa'dī. He also learnt Arabic. In the time of Ibrāhīm Sharki it is said that Jaunpur contained hundreds of colleges and mosques, and up to the time of the Emperor Shāh Jahān (1627–1658) it was still in a flourishing condition. Afterwards it declined in influence, though it still continued as a place of learning well into the eighteenth century.

Besides the efforts of ruling sovereigns there is evidence

[1] Law, pp. 80-90. [2] *Ibid.*, pp. 91–113. [3] *Ibid.*, p. 136.

that the patronage and encouragement of learning, and the foundation of colleges and schools, were also undertaken by many of the nobility and gentry. By the time, then, that the Mughal emperors began to reign in India there must have already existed a great many Muhammadan colleges and schools in various parts of India. We cannot, of course, always rely on the statements of the historians, many of whom were court favourites, and anxious to show in the best light the activities of their patrons. It seems that colleges which were called into being by royal patrons, and existed by the subsidies they allowed, easily came to nought if patronage was not continued by their successors, or in times of distress, like Taimūr's invasion. And a college does not necessarily mean a large institution. It may mean no more than a class attached to a mosque with a single teacher in charge. Moreover, it was chiefly in the capitals and other important centres that monarchs are said to have established colleges. But, even making all allowance for exaggeration, it seems quite evident that Muhammadan higher education, before the invasion of Bābar, must have been established in many important centres, and probably a large number of mosques had attached to them a *maktab*, in which pupils learnt some passages of the Korān by heart, and sometimes also the three R's. Many learned men also taught pupils in their own houses. It is all the more surprising, therefore, that the Emperor Bābar, in his interesting memoirs, says that Hindustān had no colleges. He writes [1]: 'The people of Hindustān have no good horses, no good flesh, no grapes or musk-melons, no good fruits, no ice or cold water, no good food or bread in their bazars, no baths or *colleges*, no candles, no torches, not a candlestick.' It has, indeed, been pointed out that he was speaking of Upper India,[2]

[1] Talbot's *Memoirs of Bābar*, p. 190.

[2] Mr. H. Beveridge in Introd. to *Promotion of Learning in India by Muhammadans*, p. xxv.

the only part known to him at the time, and, of course, of Muhammadan colleges, and that thus limited his statement is probably correct; but it seems evident that the fame of colleges in India could not have spread beyond its borders, and it may be, therefore, that they were not so numerous nor so flourishing as the court historians would lead us to suppose.

Bābar, the first of the Mughal emperors (1526–1530), was a man of great accomplishments, with a knowledge of Arabic, Persian, and Turkish, and a taste for poetry; but he had barely won his kingdom in India when he died at the early age of forty-eight. His son, Humāyūn (1530–1556), was, like his father, an accomplished scholar, who gave great encouragement to learned men; but he was for a long time banished from India, when his throne was occupied by Sher Shāh (1540–1545). A college was built by Humāyūn at Delhi,[1] and by Sher Shāh at Narnaul.[2] The tomb of Humāyūn also for some time had a college attached to it.[3]

Akbar (1556–1605) was the most brilliant of all the Mughal emperors, but it is remarkable that he is generally supposed to have been unable to read or write. This, indeed, has been disputed,[4] but whether it was so or not we cannot call him an uneducated man, and he was deeply interested in the work of spreading education and learning. Several Muhammadan sovereigns in India seem to have been active in founding libraries. We have already mentioned the library of three thousand volumes at Bīdar,[5] in the Bahmanī kingdom, and it was by falling from the balcony of his library that Humāyūn met his death. Akbar[6] was particularly zealous in building up a great library, and almost every day he had books from it read to him. He was a patron not only of Muhammadan

[1] Law, p. 133.
[2] *Ibid.*, p. 137.
[3] *Ibid.*, p. 134.
[4] *Ibid.*, pp. 139–142.
[5] See p. 119.
[6] For Akbar as a patron of learning, see Law, pp. 139–172.

learning but also of Hindu learning, and had a large number of Sanskrit and other books translated into Persian. Akbar, like other sovereigns, was a builder of colleges, not only at his new city of Fathpur Sīkrī, but also at Agra and other places. Colleges, it seems, were not always residential institutions, and one scholar in giving an account of himself says that he used to go twice a day, morning and evening, to a college at Delhi, although he lived two miles away.[1] Colleges also were erected by private individuals, and amongst others by Māham Anaga, who was Akbar's nurse. This lady erected a college at Delhi, the ruins of which are still to be seen. Painting, music, and caligraphy were encouraged by Akbar, as well as other fine arts.

Akbar, who in his later years was very tolerant in religious matters, made arrangements for Hindu youths to be educated at the *madrasahs* as well as Muhammadans. His great finance minister was a Hindu named Todar Mal. Todar Mal ordered all official accounts to be kept in Persian, and this regulation, by compelling many Hindus to study that language, helped the growth and development of Urdu also, and its acceptance as the *lingua franca* of a great part of India.[2]

At the new city of Fathpur Sīkrī, Akbar erected a hall called the Ibādat Kḥāna, where discussions were frequently held in his presence. Not only were the representatives of various religions invited to put forward the claims of their respective faiths, but many other debates were held on religious, philosophical, scientific, and historical questions. A matter which was discussed at one of these debates led to Akbar making a strange experiment which is not without interest to educationists.

It is said that one day it was being debated as to what was the first language of mankind. The Muhammadans declared

[1] Elliot, *Hist. of India as told by its own Historians*, vi 176.

[2] Grierson, *Literature of Hindustan*, p. 35.

that it was Arabic, the Jews said it was Hebrew, while the Brāhmans maintained that it was Sanskrit. Akbar wished to discover the truth of this matter, and so he ordered twelve new-born infants to be secured and brought up in strict seclusion by dumb nurses. Not a word was to be spoken in their hearing till they had reached twelve years of age. When the time arrived the children were brought before the royal presence, and experts in the various learned tongues were present to catch the first words which fell from the lips of the children, and to decide to which language it belonged. As might have been expected, they could not utter a word, but communicated with each other only by signs. The children were afterwards taught to speak, but with the greatest possible difficulty. This is the story as it is related by Father Catrou,[1] who based his history of the Mughal dynasty on the memoirs of the Italian Manucci, who was for forty-eight years physician to the Mughal emperors. Badaunī, the Muhammadan historian, who was unfriendly to Akbar, gives a slightly different version of the story,[2] which is simpler and perhaps nearer the truth. He says that several suckling infants were kept in a secluded place far from habitations, where they were not to hear a word spoken. Well-disciplined nurses were placed with them, who were to refrain from giving any instruction in speaking, so as to test the accuracy of the tradition which says that every one that is born is born with an inclination to religion, by ascertaining what religion and sect these infants would incline to, and, above all, what creed they would repeat. Badaunī also says that about twenty infants were thus segregated, and that after three or four years some had died, but the others were all dumb. The experiment may, indeed, appear a somewhat foolish one, and not without a shade of cruelty, but educationists may perhaps envy Akbar the power of carrving out a

[1] Banerjee's trans., p. 117.

[2] J. Talboys Wheeler, *Hist. of India*, iv. 174; Elliot, ii. 288.

psychological investigation of this kind, and wish he had used his opportunity for conducting experiments which would have been more useful.

Akbar's interest in, and care for, education is shown by a most remarkable passage in the Āīn-i-Akbarī (or institutes of Akbar). This work, which was composed by Abul Fazl, Akbar's personal friend and minister, contains a most interesting account of his administration. The following passage refers to education [1] :—

'In every country, but especially in Hindustān, boys are kept for years at school, where they learn the consonants and vowels. A great portion of the life of the students is wasted by making them read many books. His majesty orders that every schoolboy should first learn to write the letters of the alphabet, and also learn to trace their several forms. He ought to learn the shape and name of each letter, which may be done in two days, when the boy should proceed to write the joined letters. They may be practised for a week, after which the boy should learn some prose and poetry by heart, and then commit to memory some verses to the praise of God, or moral sentences, each written separately. Care is to be taken that he learns to understand everything himself, but the teacher may assist him a little. He then ought for some time to be daily practised in writing a hemistich or a verse, and will soon acquire a current hand. The teacher ought specially to look after five things, knowledge of the letters; meanings of words; the hemistich; the verse; the former lesson. If this method of teaching be adopted a boy will learn in a month, or even in a day, what it took others years to understand, so much so that people will get quite astonished. Every boy ought to read books on morals, arithmetic, the notation peculiar to arithmetic, agriculture, mensuration, geometry,

[1] Blochmann's trans., p. 278; see also Gladwin's trans., i. 223.

astronomy, physiognomy, household matters, the rules of government, medicine, logic, the tabī'ī, riyāzī, and ilāhī sciences, and history; all of which may be gradually acquired.[1] In studying Sanskrit students ought to learn the Bayākaran, Niyāī, Bedānta, and Patanjal. No one should be allowed to neglect those things which the present time requires. These regulations shed a new light on schools, and cast a bright lustre over *madrasahs*.'

This most interesting statement illustrates Akbar's great concern for education. It seems intended to bring about certain reforms in the schools, but the exact nature of those reforms is difficult to understand in the absence of information as to the state of affairs which it was intended to replace. Like many other reformers Akbar seems to have thought that too much time was spent in learning the mechanical arts of reading and writing, and he was probably trying to overcome the difficulties which the Persian character presents to the beginner. He seems to be recommending, in the first place, a quicker method of teaching these subjects. In the chapter on popular education it will be shown how in Hindu schools writing was taught before reading, and by the pupil running his pen over letters traced by the master, whereas in the Muhammadan Persian schools reading was taught before writing. Is it not possible that Akbar was impressed by the more rapid progress made in Hindu schools, in learning reading and writing, and wished to introduce these methods into Muhammadan schools also? His broad tolerance and interest in Hindus as well as Muhammadans makes this not unlikely. With regard to his regulations for learning by heart it is, again, not clear what reform is intended. It may be that

[1] 'The tabī'ī, riyāzī, and ilāhī sciences are the names of the threefold divisions of sciences. Ilāhī, or divine, sciences comprise everything connected with theology, and the means of acquiring a knowledge of God. Riyāzī sciences treat of quantity, and comprise mathematics, astronomy, music, and mechanics. Tabī'ī sciences comprehend physical sciences.'

he wished to reduce the time spent on this also, and make it more intelligent by insisting on the pupils understanding what they were learning, and writing out what they learnt. It is noteworthy that among the five things which the teacher is urged specially to look after are the meanings of words and the revision of the former lesson. Akbar evidently intended whatever was done to be done thoroughly. The injunction that 'care is to be taken that he (the pupil) learns to understand everything himself, but the teacher may assist him a little,' sounds almost like a quotation from a modern text-book on education. While, however, we must be careful not to read too much into this or any other statement of this document we can say at least that it shows that Akbar saw the need of intelligent co-operation on the part of the pupil in the work of education, and that true progress can only be made when the pupil is learning to think out his own problems. The curriculum which is put forward as suitable for 'every boy' must evidently be intended for the *madrasah* rather than for the primary schools. Even so it is a very wide one. It is to be noticed that in the earlier portion of the document Akbar laments the fact that a great portion of the life of students is wasted by making them read 'many books', and yet he here recommends the study of a very large number of subjects. But the two things are not inconsistent. The former statement evidently refers to the reading of many books without understanding them, or of books which his majesty would not consider of much practical use, as, for example, the vapid *belles lettres* in Persian. He seems, in fact, to be taking the line so often taken by practical men of affairs, and to deprecate mere book-learning as contrasted with the acquisition of practical knowledge. The curriculum which he lays down contains a preponderance of scientific subjects, but these were, no doubt, those usually taught in the *madrasahs*. We can, however, hardly suppose that any one *madrasah* taught them all, or that many students could get a thorough grasp of such a wide range of subjects. The order of subjects in Akbar's scheme seems to give a preference to those which were of practical utility, which suits the character of Akbar, who was himself an inventor and encouraged the mechanical arts. It is to be noted, however, that the subject of morals heads the list, and theology was also included. The short reference at the end of the document to Hindu education shows Akbar's interest in that also. It apparently only records what was the usual practice in teaching Sanskrit students, and the emperor would hardly have dared to work out reforms for the Brāhmanic education, but the injunction that 'no one should be allowed to neglect those things which the present time requires' may be taken as a suggestion that the practical side of education should not be neglected.

These regulations certainly bring out in a very favourable light not only Akbar's interest in and care for the education of his people, but also his attempt to make that education efficient. It is possible that Abul Fazl or other ministers of Akbar may have had a hand in framing such regulations, but it is probable that Akbar himself also had at least some part in the matter, for they suit the practical bent of his character. The question may well be asked as to how far these regulations were carried into practical effect and what was their result. There was no such thing as an education department, nor were there inspectors of schools in those days, and even supposing this document to have been circulated to all local officials and to all schools it is not unlikely that it may have, to a large extent, remained a dead letter, except by way of suggestion to the more enterprising teachers. No doubt in schools which came under the personal notice of the emperor or of any officials as interested as he was, and as anxious for reform, there may have been some notice taken of it, but it is hardly likely that the conservative traditions of the schools would have been altered very easily.

Akbar's son and successor, Jahāngīr[1] (1605–1627), was in many ways a less able sovereign than his father. He was not, however, without some predilections for learning, and he wrote, with the assistance of others, his own memoirs. He was a lover of books and paintings, and gave great encouragement to artists. Some of these he employed to illustrate his own memoirs. Agra was at this time still a great centre of learning, and the exponents of various religious faiths are said to have come to live in the city to set forth their respective creeds. In the matter of building colleges Jahāngīr was active, and it is recorded that he repaired some colleges which for thirty years had been desolate and inhabited only by birds and beasts. Jahāngīr not only repaired them, but supplied them again with teachers and pupils. He made a law that when any wealthy man died without leaving an heir his property was to escheat to the crown and be used for the repair of colleges, monasteries, and other religious buildings. Shāh Jahān's reign[2] (1627–1658) is specially famous for the erection of many fine buildings, but does not seem to be marked by any remarkable educational progress. He did not, however, reverse the policy of his predecessors in the encouragement of learning, and like them also he was a patron of music and painting and the fine arts. A college was founded at Delhi in this reign close by the great mosque of that city, and another college in Delhi was repaired and re-established. Shāh Jahān's son, Prince Dārā Shukoh, was a great scholar, with a strong leaning towards Hindu philosophy. He translated many Sanskrit works into Persian, among others the *Upanishads*.

The French traveller Bernier visited India during the reign of Shāh Jahān, and it is remarkable that he draws a most

[1] Law, pp. 173–180. [2] *Ibid.*, pp. 180–186.

unsatisfactory picture of the state of education in India. He says[1]—

'A profound and universal ignorance is the natural consequence of such a state of society as I have endeavoured to describe. Is it possible to establish in Hindustān academies and colleges properly endowed? Where shall we seek for founders? Or, should they be found, where are the scholars? Where are the individuals whose property is sufficient to support their children at colleges? or if such individuals exist who would venture to display so clear a proof of wealth? Lastly, if any persons should be tempted to commit this great imprudence, yet where are the benefices, the employments, the offices of trust and dignity, that require ability and science, and are calculated to excite the emulation and the hopes of the young student?'

When one thinks of the record of the founding of numerous colleges during the reigns of the Mughal emperors, to say nothing of those that were founded by earlier Muhammadan sovereigns, and also of the zeal for, and interest in, education shown by sovereigns like Fīrūz Shāh and Akbar, and of the mention also of educational institutions started by many private patrons, it is difficult to imagine how such a melancholy view of the state of education could have been taken by this seventeenth-century traveller. It is interesting to compare his view with that taken by the Emperor Bābar in his memoirs. Like many other visitors from the West, Bernier no doubt judged the state of affairs in India too much by European standards, and relied too much on casual observation for the formation of his opinion. But he could hardly have written such a paragraph if education had been as widespread in India as we might be tempted to suppose by the numerous references to the building of colleges. An interesting sidelight is thrown on the situation by the frequent mention of the repair of

[1] *Bernier's Travels* (Constable's trans.), p. 229.

colleges which had fallen into disuse and bad repair. Thus Jahāngīr is said to have repaired and re-established no less than thirty of such colleges which had become so ruined as to be inhabited by birds and beasts, while Shāh Jahān also did the same for a college in the royal city of Delhi; and this was subsequent to the reign of Akbar when education was so highly favoured and encouraged. It certainly looks as though some colleges were quickly deserted by tutors and scholars when the pious founder died or his interest languished. They migrated in many cases to a newer institution which offered better conditions. And it may be that in the latter part of his statement, where Bernier laments the lack of suitable employments and positions for young men who have studied, he is reflecting the opinion of some with whom he came into contact who may have given as their reason for not pursuing higher studies the lack of certainty in obtaining suitable employment when their course was completed. Brāhman education, carried on largely in secluded places and without any royal provision for its support, save the encouragement given by princes like Akbar and Dārā Shukoh, probably escaped his notice. While, therefore, we must discount a great deal the unfavourable opinion of Bernier, it will help us, on the other hand, not to over-estimate the progress of education in India even under the best of the Mughal emperors.

It was part of the policy of Aurangzīb[1] (1658–1707), who was a strict and orthodox Muhammadan, to give great encouragement to Muhammadan education. He was hard indeed on the Hindus, and in 1669 ordered the destruction of temples and the prohibition of Hindu teaching and worship at Benares and other places. He also once confiscated the buildings belonging to the Dutch in Lucknow and made them over to a Muhammadan for use as a college. Towards Muhammadan education, however, Aurangzīb showed great

[1] Law, pp. 187–193.

favour. In the *Mirāt-i-Ālam*[1] we read: 'All the mosques in the empire are repaired at the public expense. *Imāms*, criers to the daily prayers, and readers of the *khutba*, have been appointed to each of them, so that a large sum of money has been and is still laid out in these disbursements. In all the cities and towns of this extensive country, pensions and allowances and lands have been given to learned men and professors, and stipends have been fixed for scholars according to their abilities and qualifications.' Besides these stipends for professors and students Aurangzīb founded a large number of colleges and schools. He sent orders to the provinces of Gujarāt and other places that all Muhammadan students were to be given pecuniary help. He also took steps to have the Bohras of Gujarāt educated, and for this purpose teachers were appointed and monthly examinations were to be held, the results of which were to be reported to the emperor. Colleges were also erected in this reign by private individuals, and at this time Sialkot, which began to be a place of learning about the time of Akbar, came into prominence as an educational centre. Aurangzīb added to the Imperial Library many Muhammadan theological works. Though narrow in his literary and theological outlook he was not without learning, and he not only knew his mother tongue of Turkish, but could read and write Arabic and Persian with great facility. He had learnt the Korān by heart and also the Hādīs, or traditions, and was well versed in Muhammadan theology.

We learn that it was the practice with young princes when they reached the age of four years, four months, and four days, to perform the '*maktab* ceremony.' The child was seated in the schoolhouse and formally handed over to tutors for his instruction to commence. We read of this ceremony being performed in the case of Humāyūn, and it is also said to have taken place in the case of Akbar, although there is a doubt

[1] Elliot, vii. 159.

about his literacy. This custom seems also to have become common amongst other Muhammadan boys, and is still in use in India.[1] The young princes were first taught to read and write their mother tongue. With regard to their education Catrou, following Manucci, says [2]: 'Whilst the princes remain in the harem, under the eye of their father, a eunuch is charged with their education. They are taught to read and sometimes to write in Arabic and in Persian. Their bodies are formed to military exercises, and they are instructed in the principles of equity. They are taught to decide rationally upon subjects of dispute which occur, or on suppositious suits at law. Finally they are instructed in the Muhammadan religion, and in the interests of the nation, which they may be called one day to govern.' There is an incident in the life of Aurangzīb which throws a valuable sidelight on the education of the young Muhammadan princes, and also gives to us that monarch's views upon the subject. It is related to us by the French traveller Bernier, who got a report of the incident from one who was present.[3]

Aurangzīb's old tutor, Mulla Shāh, hearing of his pupil's success in gaining the throne, went to visit him, expecting reward and advancement. For three months Aurangzīb refused to see him, and when at last he saw him he spoke as follows: 'Pray, what is your pleasure with me, Mulla-jī? Do you pretend that I ought to exalt you to the first honours of the State? Let us examine your title to any mark of distinction. I do not deny you would possess such a title if you had filled my young mind with suitable instruction. Show me a well-educated youth and I will say that it is doubtful who has the stronger claim to his gratitude, his father or his tutor. But what was the knowledge I derived under your tuition?

[1] In the Panjab the '*maktab* ceremony' is called '*bismi' llah*'
[2] Catrou, p. 288.
[3] *Bernier's Travels*, pp. 155 ff.

You taught us that the whole of Franguistan (Europe) was no more than some inconsiderable island, of which the most powerful monarch was formerly the king of Portugal, then he of Holland, and afterwards the king of England. In regard to the other sovereigns of Franguistan, such as the king of France and him of Andalusia, you told me that they resembled our petty *rājas*, and that the potentates of Hindustān eclipsed the glory of all other kings; that they alone were Humāyūns, Akbars, Jahāngīrs or Shāh Jahāns; the Happy, the Great, the Conquerors of the World and the Kings of the World[1]; and that Persia, Usbec, Kashgar, Tartary, and Cathay, Pegu, Siam, China, trembled at the names of the kings of the Indies. Admirable geographer! deeply-read historian! Was it not incumbent upon my preceptor to make me acquainted with the distinguishing features of every nation of the earth; its resources and strength; its mode of warfare, its manners, religion, form of government, and wherein its interests principally consist; and by a regular course of historical reading to render me familiar with the origin of states, their progress and decline; the events, accidents, or errors, owing to which such great changes and mighty revolutions have been effected? Far from having imparted to me a profound and comprehensive knowledge of the history of mankind, scarcely did I learn from you the names of my ancestors, the renowned founders of this empire. You kept me in total ignorance of their lives, of the events which preceded, and the extraordinary talents that enabled them to achieve their extensive conquests. A familiarity with the languages of surrounding nations may be indispensable in a king; but you would teach me to read and write Arabic, doubtless conceiving that you placed me under an everlasting obligation for sacrificing so large a portion of time to the study of a language wherein no one can hope to become proficient without ten or twelve years of close application.

[1] These are the meanings of the names of these sovereigns.

Forgetting how many important subjects ought to be embraced in the education of a prince, you acted as if it were chiefly necessary that he should possess great skill in grammar, and such knowledge as belongs to a doctor of law; and thus did you waste the precious hours of my youth in the dry, unprofitable, and never-ending task of learning words.' Bernier goes on to say that some of the learned men, either wishing to flatter the monarch and add energy to his speech, or actuated by jealousy of the *mulla*, affirm that the king's reproof did not end here, but that, when he had spoken for a short time on other subjects, he continued his speech as follows:—

'Were you not aware that it is during the period of infancy, when the memory is commonly so retentive, that the mind may receive a thousand wise precepts; and be easily furnished with such valuable instructions as will elevate it with lofty conceptions, and render the individual capable of glorious deeds? Can we repeat our prayers, or acquire a knowledge of law and of the sciences only through the medium of Arabic? May not our devotions be offered up as acceptably, and solid information communicated as easily, in our mother tongue? You gave my father, Shāh Jahān, to understand that you instructed me in philosophy; and, indeed, I have a perfect remembrance of your having, during several years, harassed my brain with idle and foolish propositions, the solution of which yield no satisfaction to the mind—propositions which seldom enter into the business of life; wild and extravagant reveries conceived with great labour and forgotten as soon as conceived; whose only effect is to fatigue and ruin the intellect, and to render a man headstrong and insufferable. O yes, you caused me to devote the most valuable years of my life to your favourite hypotheses, or systems, and when I left you, I could boast of no greater attainment in the sciences than the use of many obscure and uncouth terms, calculated to discourage, confound, and appal a youth of the most masculine understanding; terms invented to cover the vanity and ignorance of pretenders to philosophy; of men who, like yourself, would impose the belief that they transcend others of their species in wisdom, and that their dark and ambiguous jargon conceals many profound mysteries known only to themselves. If you had taught me that philosophy which adapts the mind to reason, and will not suffer it to rest satisfied with anything short of the most solid arguments; if you had inculcated lessons which elevate the soul and fortify it against the assaults of fortune, tending to produce that envi-able equanimity which is neither insolently elated by pros-perity, nor basely depressed by adversity, if you had made me acquainted with the nature of men; accustomed me always to refer to first principles, and given me a sublime and adequate conception of the universe, and of the order and regular motion of its parts; if such, I say, had been the nature of the philo-sophy imbibed under your tuition, I should be more indebted to you than Alexander was to Aristotle, and should consider it my duty to bestow a very different reward on you than Aristotle received from that Prince. Answer me, sycophant, ought you not to have instructed me on one point at least, so essential to be known by a king; namely, on the reciprocal duties between the sovereign and his subjects? Ought you not also to have foreseen that I might, at some future period, be compelled to contend with my brothers, sword in hand, for the crown, and for my very existence? Such, as you must well know, has been the fate of the children of almost every king of Hindustān. Did you ever instruct me in the art of war, how to besiege a town, or draw up an army in battle array? Happy for me that I consulted wiser heads than thine on these subjects! Go. Withdraw to thy village. Hence-forth let no person know either who thou art, or what is become of thee.'

Making all due allowance for any embellishments added consciously or unconsciously by Bernier, this pronouncement upon the subject of education is most interesting and noteworthy. It makes very little difference whether part of it came from Aurangzīb's counsellors or not, for taking it as it stands it gives the view of Muhammadan education held by the seventeenth-century men of affairs in India and their criticism of its defects. Aurangzīb's part in this pronouncement is all the more remarkable from the fact of his being an orthodox Muhammadan, who himself had a good knowledge of Arabic and delighted to read and study Muhammadan theological works. He was not a broad-minded student of human nature like Akbar, whose philosophic outlook was a species of eclecticism. But narrow as were Aurangzīb's views on some questions he was a shrewd and able ruler, and saw the need of a more satisfactory education than he himself had received. He was not objecting to the theological basis of his education, but to the pedantry and formalism which characterized it. He objects to the mere learning of words and terms without the power to understand or use them, and which had no vital connection with the world outside the school. The study of Arabic must have become as formal as the study of the classics had become in the schools of seventeenth-century Europe, and Aurangzīb objects to the wasting of so much time in obtaining mere skill in grammar. We have seen how Akbar seems to have placed a great emphasis on the teaching of scientific subjects. Aurangzīb appears to be pleading for a broad humanism in which history, geography, and the languages of the surrounding nations would have a large place. The formation of high ideals, and of such habits of thought and action as would enable the pupil to meet all the difficulties of life with wisdom and courage are also set forth as necessary to a good education. The desirability of connecting the education given with the vocation to be followed by the pupil in after-life is another educational aim which Aurangzīb proposes. All this has the appearance of being very modern, and it is of the highest interest to find these two monarchs, Akbar and Aurangzīb, who are amongst the greatest rulers of India, and who were in so many ways different from each other in character and outlook on life, each advocating some of those very reforms in education which are being called for loudly at the present time. The only pity is that neither of them seems to have gone very far in giving practical effect to the educational ideals which they set forth.

After the death of Aurangzīb the glory of the Mughal empire began rapidly to wane, and the efforts made by emperors or private individuals to erect and endow educational institutions became much more rare. There is record of two *madrasahs* having been founded at Delhi during the reign of Aurangzīb's successor, Bahādur Shāh[1] (1707–1712). One of these buildings erected by Ghāzī-ud-dīn, an officer of Aurangzīb, is still in existence though no longer used as a college. It is typical of many such buildings, having in the same enclosure the college, a mosque, and the tomb of the founder.[2] It was closed in 1793 for want of funds. The invasion of Nādir Shāh, which took place in 1739 and resulted in the sack of Delhi, must have been a great set-back to educational progress. Among other things the Imperial Library, which had been built up by the interest of many sovereigns, was carried away by Nādir Shāh to Persia.[3]

With regard to the education of women[4] it was just as much restricted amongst Muhammadans as amongst Hindus. The pardah system, which shut up all Muhammadan women, except young girls, in seclusion, made their education a matter of great difficulty even where it may have been desired, which

[1] Law, p. 194.
[2] Fanshawe's *Delhi Past and Present*, p. 64.
[3] Law, p. 198. [4] *Ibid.*, pp. 200 ff.

does not seem to have been often the case. We have evidence[1] that sometimes young girls were taught in schools as well as boys, but their leaving school at a very early age must have prevented their education being carried very far. It seems that sometimes in the harem of kings or nobles some attempt was made to give education to the ladies who lived within, and some of them attained to great distinction. Ghiyās-ud-dīn, who was ruler of Mālwā from 1469–1500, is said[2] to have appointed school-mistresses for the ladies of his harem, and Akbar also made a similar arrangement for his household, and certain rooms were set apart at Fathpur Sīkrī for this purpose. Razīya, who sat on the throne of Delhi after her father Altamsh, was an educated princess and patronized men of learning. The daughter of Bābar, Gul-Badan Begam, wrote the *Humāyūn Nāmah*, or memoirs of her brother Humāyūn. It is said also that she had her own library and used to collect books. The niece of Humāyūn, who became one of Akbar's wives, wrote poems in Persian. The nurse of Akbar, Māham Anaga, mentioned above,[3] was an educated lady. Nūr Jahān, the wife of Jahāngīr, who helped her husband to rule his empire, and her niece Mumtāz Mahal, who was the favourite wife of Shāh Jahān, and in memory of whom he erected the Tāj Mahal at Agra, were both educated. So also was Jahānārā Begam, the eldest daughter of Shāh Jahān, and she had been instructed by a learned lady named Satiunnisā. The eldest daughter of Aurangzīb, Zībunnisā Begam, was acquainted with both Persian and Arabic. It is probable that many other royal and noble ladies, whose names have not been recorded, also received some education behind the pardah, but even so they were few compared with the great mass of Muhammadan women who received no education at all, except a domestic training in the performance of the duties of the household.

[1] See Ja'far Sharif, *Qānūn-i-Islām*, p. 32.
[2] Ferishta, iv. 237.
[3] See p. 122.

It is very difficult to estimate the extent of Muhammadan education in early times. As we have seen, the Emperor Bābar, and at a later date the traveller Bernier, give a very unfavourable view of the extent of education in India. But their opinions cannot be accepted without considerable qualification, for we have, on the other hand, the record of the building of numerous *madrasahs* and of the existence of important educational centres, at places like Delhi, Agra, and Jaunpur. The Muhammadan population was, no doubt, in many places largely a town population as it is to-day (except in the Panjāb), and it was in the cities of importance that *madrasahs* are said to have been established. We have no idea as to the average number of students attending a college. Probably this varied considerably from just a few pupils with one teacher, to a large number with many teachers in the more important places. Probably most mosques had attached to them, if not a *madrasah,* then a *maktab*, or primary school. All Muhammadan boys were supposed to attend a *maktab* in order that they might at least learn the portions of the Korān required for the Muhammadan daily devotions, but we cannot be sure that they always did so. The content of the education given in the *maktabs* must have been very different in different places. When the Muhammadan boy begins to speak he should be taught to repeat the Muhammadan article of belief (the *kalima*). After that certain prescribed verses from the Korān have to be learnt by heart. At about seven years of age he begins to learn the Korān, and receives instructions in religious precepts and usages. This seems to be the minimum education given in a *maktab*. In some cases, however, reading and writing were also taught and some elementary arithmetic. To this might be added legends of prophets and anecdotes of Muhammadan saints, and perhaps some selections from poets. The teaching of Persian must have begun at some time during the Muhammadan rule, and

Persian schools became widespread, as this language was required by those who wished for employment in government service. These schools are referred to again later in the chapter on popular education. With regard to modern survivals of Korān schools in India, the *Quinquennial Review of Education*[1] quotes Mr. de la Fosse as saying that these 'are usually attached to a mosque . . . the scholars commence by studying the Arabic alphabet, and as soon as they can read are made to recite *suras*, or chapters of the Korān. Neither writing nor arithmetic is taught. So far as my experience goes instruction is usually confined to reading and memorizing, but sometimes an attempt is also made to explain the meaning of what is read. This, however, is rare.'

The content of the education given in the *madrasahs* also must have varied in different places. Probably not every school taught all the subjects, and pupils selected such as they wished to study. Adam, in his report on education in Bengal (1835–1838), says with regard to the *madrasahs*[2]: 'In the Arabic schools the course of study takes a much wider range. The grammatical works are numerous, systematized, and profound; complete courses of reading on rhetoric, logic, and law are embraced; the external observances and fundamental doctrines of Islām, and Ptolemy on astronomy in translation, are not unknown; other branches of natural philosophy are also taught; and the whole course is crowned by the perusal of treatises on metaphysics, deemed the highest attainment of the instructed scholar.' It is interesting to compare this list of subjects with those which formed the curriculum of the universities of Europe in the Middle Ages. We find a very close correspondence between them. The 'Seven Liberal Arts' all appear except dialectic and music. Dialectic was probably largely covered by rhetoric. Music did not have the same

[1] *Quinquennial Review of Education in India*, 1907–1912, p. 272.
[2] *Adam's Reports*, p. 215.

connection with religious services as in Christian Europe, and therefore was not of such importance from the religious point of view. That it was cultivated we know from the encouragement given to it by Akbar and other sovereigns, though Aurangzīb could not tolerate it. The higher studies of mediæval European universities, theology, law, and medicine, also appear in this list, except medicine. Medicine was, however, studied, and even at the present time Muhammadan *hakīms*, or physicians learned in the ancient medical lore, practise in India. Medicine appears in Akbar's list of studies. Law was, of course, more closely connected with theology than in Europe, for in Islām it is based on the Korān and the Traditions, whereas in Europe it was the non-christian Roman law that was the basis of studies. We know that at a certain period in the Middle Ages Muhammadan learning in the West was full of intellectual vigour, and in many ways was the means of stimulating thought and mental activity amongst students in Europe. But the zenith of its influence was passed before it became widespread in India, and it is perhaps for this reason amongst others that it never attained to such an excellence and fame in India as in more western lands. The criticisms of Aurangzīb, as well as the statement of Adam, seems to show that Muhammadan learning in India, like the mediæval learning of Europe, had become formal and scholastic, with a strong emphasis on grammar, and having as its climax the discussion of dry, abstract and metaphysical trivialities. That it often included more than this, as did the mediæval education of Europe, we may be quite sure. Science of some kind was studied, and literature and history were also taught. History was, in fact, a very favourite subject amongst the Muhammadans of India, and the large number of historical works written by Muhammadan writers is in striking contrast with the paucity of Hindu historical literature. The critical and impartial spirit which modern scientific historians seek to cultivate is indeed lacking, nor could we really expect to find it in those days. We shall not be very far wrong if we say that the state of Muhammadan learning in India was very much the same as that of learning in Europe before the introduction of printing. In the matter of the arts and crafts there was little difference, if any, between the training of the Hindu and Muhammadan craftsman, and this subject has been dealt with in the chapter on the training of special classes of the community. In method also there was probably not much essential difference between the Hindu and Muhammadan education. Rote learning was given a large place, and the principal aim of the teacher was to pass on to the pupil the learned traditions which he himself had received.

It must be remembered that Muhammadan education was at best confined, to a very large extent, to that minority of the population which embraced the religion of Islam. At first this minority was very small, and it has never included more than about one-fifth of the population. For centuries the Muhammadans were little more than an armed garrison in a foreign land, and though many inhabitants of India joined the Muhammadan religion the learned class of the Brāhmans held firmly to their old faith. In spite of this, however, the extent and influence of the Muhammadan education in India was by no means inconsiderable. Its fluctuating and uncertain character was very largely the result of despotic rule which indulged in sudden impulses and afforded no certainty of the continuance of any new undertaking, as shown in the many Delhis which were built and deserted. The same happened in the case of the *madrasahs*. Moreover the poverty of the country and the rapacity of officials stifled the popular demand for education. The *maktab* attached to the mosque was probably the most permanent of Muhammadan educational institutions in India, and those of them which taught Persian, a language which was required for official use, were resorted to even by

Hindus who wished to acquire this language, and thus had an influence on a considerable proportion of the population. They formed part of that system of popular elementary education which will be described in a later chapter.[1]

[1] With regard to schools of the old type still existing, the *Quinquennial Review* for 1907–1912 reports that in 1912 there were 1446 Arabic and Persian schools, and 8288 Korān schools, as against 2051 and 10,504 in 1907. Pupils had also decreased.

CHAPTER V

POPULAR ELEMENTARY EDUCATION

We have already seen how from the earliest times we can trace the presence of an extensive educational system in India. In the case of both Hindus and Muhammadans this was connected closely with religion. Hindu education was in the hands of the Brāhmans and mainly intended for them, though the other higher castes were not excluded. Muhammadan education centred round the mosque and was supervised by the maulvis. Certain classes of the community also had their own special forms of education.

Side by side, however, with these systems there grew up at some time and in most parts of India a popular system of elementary education which was open generally to all comers. It must have arisen to supply a popular demand for instruction in reading, writing, and arithmetic, and was made use of chiefly by the trading and agricultural classes.

At the renewal of the charter of the East India Company in 1813 a lakh of rupees was ordered to be set apart every year for the promotion of literature and education This led to the various local governments of India making inquiries as to indigenous education. The result of those inquiries has been that we have a valuable record of education in India as it existed before Western influences had seriously affected it, and before those modern developments took place which have had such a far-reaching influence upon India. The inquiry for the Madras Presidency was carried out in 1822–1826; that for Bombay in 1823–1828. It is, however, the report of William Adam, who was appointed by Lord William Bentinck to carry out the inquiry in the Bengal Presidency, that is the most full of interest. It was published in 1835–1838, and throws most valuable light on the state of education in India at that time. In order to get an intensive rather than merely an extensive view of the situation, Adam did not attempt to survey the whole province, but rather to choose typical districts in various parts of the presidency and make a thorough examination into the existing state of affairs. Besides the Hindu *tols* and Muhammadan *madrasahs*, which were places of higher learning, there were found Hindu *pāthśālas* and Muhammadan *maktabs*.

The *pāthśālas* existed in all the larger villages as well as in the towns. The teacher and scholars numbering usually about a dozen or twenty met in the early morning under a tree in the village or in the shade of a verandah. Sometimes a temple shed or other building might be set apart for their use. The teachers were mostly Kayasths (the writer caste).[1] The teaching of reading, writing, and accounts was considered a proper occupation for that caste, whereas Brāhmans, Vaidyas, and Kshatriyas were supposed to degrade themselves by such an occupation. There were, however, some Brāhman teachers, and many other castes were represented amongst the teachers, even those of the lowest castes. In Burdwān Adam found two teachers who were lepers.[2] There were no regular fees, but the teachers received presents averaging about Rs.4 or Rs.5 a month.[3] They often eked out their income by farming or trade.[4] Among the scholars also there were a very large number of castes represented,[5] including some of those

[1] *Adam's Reports*, p. 158.
[2] *Ibid.*, p. 168.
[3] *Ibid.*, p. 160.
[4] *Ibid.*, p. 168.
[5] *Ibid.*, p. 160.

considered 'untouchable' by the higher castes. Brāhmans and Kayasths predominated. The age of the scholars was from about five or six to sixteen. The aim of the schools was strictly utilitarian, and Adam laments the neglect of moral instruction.[1] The curriculum included reading, writing, the composition of letters and elementary arithmetic and accounts, either commercial or agricultural or both. Very few text-books were in use, and those that were used were often most unsuitable, such as a reading-book containing an account of the amours of the god Kṛishna with his cowherd mistress Rādhā.[2] There were four stages of instruction. In the first period the scholar was taught to form letters on the ground with a small stick. This period usually lasted about ten days. In the next period the master traced letters on a palm leaf with an iron style. The scholar then traced over the letters with a reed pen and charcoal ink, which easily rubs out. This process was repeated over and over on the same leaf till the scholar no longer needed a copy to guide him. Then he practised on another leaf. He was afterwards exercised in writing and pronouncing the compound consonants, which in most Indian languages are modified when written together. Then practice was given in the combination of vowels and consonants, and this led on to the common names of persons. In the third period the palm leaf was replaced by the larger plantain leaf. The scholar now began to learn the composition of the simplest forms of letters. He was taught the connection of words in sentences and to distinguish literary from colloquial forms of speech. The rules of arithmetic now began with addition and subtraction. But multiplication and division were not taught as separate rules. These were effected by addition and subtraction, aided by multiplication tables which extend to twenty. The multiplication table was repeated aloud by the whole school once every morning. After

[1] Adam, p. 101. [2] *Ibid.*, pp. 98 ff.

this the pupil began to learn commercial or agricultural accounts or both. When the scholar reached the fourth period he received more advanced instruction in accounts and began the composition of business letters, petitions, grants, and similar productions. Paper now began to be used for writing, and after this had been used for about a year the scholars were considered as qualified to engage in the unassisted perusal of Bengali works like the *Rāmāyaṇa* and *Manasa Mangal*.

It is to be noted that in learning, writing came before reading. Except for the united repetition of multiplication tables and exercises of that kind, the instruction was individual, and monitors were commonly chosen from among the more advanced scholars to help those at a more elementary stage of instruction. Dr. Andrew Bell got his idea of the monitorial system from what he had seen in indigenous schools in India.

An account given by William Ward in his *View of the Hindoos* presents us with a similar picture of these indigenous schools in Bengal.[1] 'Almost all the larger villages in Bengal contain common schools, where a boy learns his letters by writing them, never by pronouncing the alphabet as in Europe. He first writes them on the ground; next with an iron style or a reed on a palm leaf; and next on a green plantain leaf. After the simple letters he writes the compounds, then the names of men, villages, animals, etc., and then the figures. While employed in writing on leaves all the scholars stand up twice a day with a monitor at their head, and repeat the numerical tables, ascending from a unit to four, and from four to twenty, from twenty to eighty, and from eighty to 1280; and during school hours they write on the palm leaf the strokes by which these numbers are defined. They next commit to memory an addition table and count from one to a hundred; and after this, on green plantain

[1] Ward, vol. i. pp. 160 ff.

leaves, they write easy sums in addition and subtraction of money; multiplication, and then reduction of money, measures, etc. The Hindu measures are all reducible to the weight, beginning with *rattīs* and ending with *manas* (maunds). The elder boys, as the last course at these schools, learn to write common letters, agreements, etc. The Hindu schools begin early in the morning and continue till nine or ten o'clock; after taking some refreshment at home the scholars return about three and continue till dark. Masters punish with cane or rod, or a truant is compelled to stand on one leg holding up a brick in each hand or to have his arms stretched out till completely tired. Masters are generally respectable Śūdras, but occasionally Brāhmans.'

In the Report of the Education Commission of 1882 there is an account of an indigenous primary school in the Bombay Presidency which belongs, of course, to a later date but gives a similar picture.[1] 'The ordinary daily routine of a Hindu indigenous school is nearly the same in all parts of the Presidency. Each morning at about six o'clock the Pantoji, who is in some cases a Brāhman, and the priest of many of the families whose children attend the school, goes round the village and collects his pupils. This process usually occupies some time. At one house the pupil has to be persuaded to come to school; at another the parents have some special instructions to give the master regarding the refractoriness of their son; at a third he is asked to administer chastisement on the spot. As soon as he has collected a sufficient number of his pupils he takes them to the school. For the first half-hour a *Bhupali*, or invocation to the sun, Saraswatī, Ganapati, or some other deity, is chanted by the whole school. After this the boys who can write trace the letters of their *kittas*, or copy slips, with a dry pen, the object of this exercise being to give free play to the fingers and wrist, and to accustom them

[1] *Bombay Report*, p. 65.

to the sweep of the letters. When the tracing lesson is over, the boys begin to write copies; and the youngest children, who have been hitherto merely looking on, are taken in hand either by the master's son or by one of the elder pupils. The master himself generally confines his attention to one or two of the oldest pupils, and to those whose instruction he has stipulated to finish within a given time. All the pupils are seated in one small room or verandah, and the confusion of sounds, which arises from three or four sets of boys reading and shouting out their tables all at the same moment, almost baffles description.'

In the Madras Presidency these schools[1] are known as *pyal* schools. The *pyal* is a kind of bench or platform about three feet high and three feet broad, which is built against the wall of most houses in South India, and has in front a raised pavement or *koradu*. On the *pyal* visitors are received, the family sleep in the hot season, and it has many other uses also. For the village school a *pyal* is usually lent by the headman of the village. The scholars sit on the *pyal*, leaving the *koradu* for the teacher and for their own passage. The main purpose of these *pyal* schools, before modern developments in education reformed them or pushed them out, was to give instruction in the three R's, but of arithmetic only the simplest elements were taught. A great deal of time was spent in construing and memorizing beautiful but obscure poems, written in the 'high' dialect (which differs not only from the colloquial, but even from the modern literary dialect). The average number of children was about twenty-one, and the school had no apparatus except the sandy ground, certain small blackboards, and some *kajan* leaves for writing. A sort of discipline was maintained by a constant and often severe use of the cane. Unruly or truant boys

[1] See article in *Indian Antiquary* for Feb., 1873, p. 52, by C. E. Gover, from which this account is taken.

were coerced by punishments that partook of torture. The teacher was usually a Brāhman. When a new scholar was to be received into the school the teacher and his scholars came to his house and he was handed over to the teacher by his parents. Various religious and other ceremonies were performed, and amongst other things the master made the new pupil repeat the whole alphabet three times, taught him a prayer to Gaṇeśa, and guided his hand in writing in a flat vessel of rice the name of Vishnu or Śiva. The pay of the teacher might be as much as Rs.15 to Rs.25 a month in the case of pupils whose parents were wealthy; but in *pyal* schools for poorer boys his emoluments only amounted to Rs.5 to Rs.10 a month. The pay of the teacher was received not only by regular monthly fees, but by certain customary presents on festivals and other occasions. Besides learning the three R's, a pupil obtained a knowledge, though generally a very unintelligent one, of about four or five of the great classics of the Tamil or the Telugu language. These books being also the moral code of the people, had value from the point of view of moral training. Some of these books, which had been printed in cheap editions, were in the hands of the scholars, but very often only the teacher possessed the books. Writing was taught in close connection with reading, and the pupil began his writing lessons when he commenced the alphabet. The alphabet was learned by writing with the finger on the sandy ground. Later he began to write with a pencil on a kind of small blackboard or slate (called a *palaka*), the surface of which was prepared from rice and charcoal. Then he had the privilege eventually of writing either with an iron style on *kajan* leaves, or with a reed pen on paper. Trading or agricultural accounts were taught as well as the composition of notes-of-hand, leases, agreements, etc., and the reading of the vernacular current hand. Education began usually at the age of five years. School commenced at about six o'clock in the morning. In the afternoon of each school day the pupil copied the next day's lesson on his *palaka*, and showed it to the master, who corrected it and heard him read it two or three times. The pupil then took it home and learnt it by heart for repetition to the teacher next morning.

Thus in various parts of India we find that there were existing popular elementary schools having the same general features though differing in some details.

It is interesting to compare with the above accounts a picture given to us of a school in South India by a traveller, Pietra della Valle, who visited India in 1623.[1]

In the mean time, while the burthens were getting in order, I entertained myself in the Porch of the Temple, beholding little boys learning arithmetic after a strange manner, which I will here relate. They were four, and having all taken the same lesson from the master, in order to get that same by heart and repeat likewise their former lessons and not forget them, one of them singing musically with a certain continu'd tone (which hath the force of making deep impression in the memory) recited part of the lesson; as for example, "One by itself makes one"; and whilst he was thus speaking he writ down the same number, not with any kind of pen, nor on paper, but (not to spend paper in vain) with his finger on the ground, the pavement being for that purpose strew'd all over with very fine sand; after the first had writ what he sung, all the rest sung and writ down the same thing together. Then the first boy sung and writ down another part of the lesson; as, for example, "Two by itself makes two", which all the rest repeated in the same manner, and so forward in order. When the pavement was full of figures they put them out with the hand, and if need were, strew'd it with new sand from a little heap which they had before them wherewith

[1] *Travels of P. della Valle* (Hakluyt Society), ii. 227.

to write further. And thus they did as long as the exercise continu'd, in which manner likewise, they told me, they learnt to read and write without spoiling paper, pens, or ink, which certainly is a pretty way.'

This widespread vernacular elementary education existed side by side with the Sanskrit schools. and there was no mutual dependence or connection between them. The former existed for the trading and commercial classes, and the latter for the religious and the learned. In the case of Muhammadan education, however, we find that there was a close connection between the Arabic schools of higher learning, or *madrasahs*, and the Persian schools or *maktabs*. The latter corresponded to the Hindu vernacular schools. Urdu was the current language amongst the Muhammadans, but this vernacular was not used as the medium of instruction. Urdu is written with Persian characters, and contains a large number of Persian words, but was considered as a patois unfit to be used as a language in the schools. Its place was taken by Persian, which had been made the court language by the Muhammadan Emperors, and continued to be used as such till 1835. A knowledge of Persian was therefore necessary to obtain an appointment in the Government service, and the Persian schools were attended by Hindus as well as Muhammadans, especially by Hindus of the Brāhman and Kayasth castes. Most of the teachers were Muhammadans, and Adam considered that as a class they were superior to the Bengali and Hindi teachers.[1] They were, however, more dependent for their support on single families or individual patrons. A few of them were also Arabic teachers, and possessed high qualifications. Their emoluments, as a rule, amounted to Rs.5 to Rs.7 a month. The subjects studied included elementary grammatical works and forms of correspondence, and popular poems and tales were read. Occasionally

[1] *Adam's Reports*, p. 215.

a work on rhetoric or a treatise on medicine or theology was studied. The *Gulistān* of Sa'dī was a very favourite text-book. Sections of the Korān were learned by heart, and the schools had a more religious connection than the Hindu vernacular schools, but Adam did not consider them morally superior to the Hindu schools.[1] The Hindu schools were vernacular and commercial; but the Muhammadan schools were also to some extent literary and philological, and employed a learned language. Printed works were not used, but manuscripts were in constant use. In contra-distinction to the Hindu vernacular schools, reading was taught before writing. Elegant penmanship was much cultivated. Adam also found some schools in which elementary Arabic was taught, but these existed merely to give the boys that knowledge of certain portions of the Korān which is necessary for Muhammadans. They taught mere names and forms and sounds, and it was considered sufficient for the boys to be able to repeat the required portions without understanding them.[2] Some of the teachers did not pretend to be able even to sign their names. There were also a few schools in which both Persian and Bengali were taught.

Besides the instruction in the schools there were also a certain number of children receiving instruction at home. William Ward says,[3] 'Hindu women are unable to teach their children their first lessons, but a father may frequently be seen teaching his child to write the alphabet when five years old'. Rich men often employed a tutor to teach their children, and when other children were admitted to share in this instruction it sometimes grew into a school. Girls, as a rule, received no education; but daughters of Rājput nobles or of *zamīndārs* often received a limited education from their fathers or family priests.

[1] *Adam's Reports*, p. 102.

[2] See also p. 140 above, where the report of Mr. de la Fosse on modern Korān schools is quoted.

[3] Ward, i. 160.

There was then, before the British Government took over control of education in India, a widespread, popular, indigenous system. It was not confined to one or two provinces, but was found in various parts of India, though some districts were more advanced than others. In the inquiry made for the Madras Presidency in 1822–6, it was calculated that rather less than one-sixth of the boys of school-going age received education of some sort.[1] In the similar inquiry made for the Bombay Presidency (1823–8) the number of boys under instruction was put down as about one in eight.[2] In one of the districts in Bengal, where Adam carried out his inquiry, he found [3] 13·2 per cent. of the whole male population receiving instruction. In another district he found 9 per cent. of all children of school-going age under instruction. William Ward says,[4] that it was supposed that about one-fifth of the male population of Bengal could read. In some parts of India the number under instruction would probably be less than in the three provinces mentioned. Widespread, therefore, as elementary education was, it did not include a very large proportion even of the male population, and amongst females of course it hardly existed at all.

An important question which arises with regard to this system of popular elementary education is, 'When did it begin?' We have seen that it was in full swing at the beginning of the nineteenth century when investigations were carried out by the Governments of Bengal, Bombay, and Madras, in various parts of India. But how far back can it be traced?

The Brāhman authorities, like the *Sūtras* and the Code of Manu, have no reference to any form of literary education

[1] See *Madras Report for Ed. Com.*, 1882.
[2] F. W. Thomas, *Hist. and Prospects of Brit. Ed. in India*, ch. i.
[3] Adam, pp. 117, 232.
[4] Ward, ii. 503.

outside of the Brāhmanical schools. But silence in works of this kind is not certain evidence that facilities for primary education did not exist, and the Brāhmans may have had reasons for wishing to ignore any forms of education which were not in their own hands. The duties of Vaiśyas, as outlined in Manu, included, as we have noticed,[1] such things as a knowledge of measures and weights, of probable profit and loss on merchandise, of the languages of men, of the manner of keeping goods, and the rules of purchase and sale. Part of this knowledge at least was probably learnt in the course of business, being passed on from father to son, but it is quite conceivable that even in very early times some merchants or others may have employed a teacher, or founded a small school, for the instruction of their sons in the elements of these subjects.[2] There is, at any rate, evidence to show that the knowledge of reading and writing was fairly widespread in India long before the time of Manu.

Writing was introduced into India about 800 B.C., and the elaboration of the Brāhmī script was completed by about 500 B.C. or even earlier.[3] A Buddhist tract called the *Sīlas*, which dates from about 450 B.C.,[4] gives a list of children's games. One of these is called *Akkharikā* (Lettering), which is explained as 'Guessing at letters traced in the air, or on a playfellow's back'. Such a game amongst children seems to show that the knowledge of the alphabet was prevalent at least amongst a certain section of the community, perhaps those who belonged to the trading and commercial classes, for it is they who would have the greatest need for a knowledge of reading and writing, and neither the Brāhman nor the Buddhist sacred books seem to have been committed to

[1] See p. 72.
[2] For present-day 'Mahājani schools', see p. 73.
[3] J. G. Bühler, *Indian Palæography*, p. 17.
[4] Rhys Davids, *Buddhist India*, p. 108.

writing till a very much later date. The ancient writers Nearchus and Q. Curtius, in the last quarter of the fourth century B.C., refer to the custom of the Indians of writing letters on cloth and bark; and Megasthenes, at a slightly later date, speaks of the use of milestones to indicate distances and halting-places on the high-roads.[1] In another passage, however, Megasthenes relates that judicial cases in India were decided according to unwritten laws, and that the Indians knew no letters. Taking these passages together it seems that at that time writing was used for public or private notifications, but that it had not begun to be used for the purposes of literature. It is then probable that the knowledge and use of writing, though widespread, was confined to the commercial and official classes, but this does not necessarily imply the existence of schools for teaching these arts.

In the *Mahāvagga* there is an interesting passage which is translated as follows[2]:—

'At that time there was in Rājagaha a company of seventeen boys, friends of each other; young Upāli was first among them. Now Upāli's father and mother thought: "How will Upāli after our death live a life of ease and without pain? If Upāli could learn writing (*lekhā*), he would after our death live a life of ease and without pain." But then Upāli's father and mother thought again: "If Upāli learns writing his fingers will become sore. But if Upāli could learn arithmetic (*gaṇanā*), he would after our death live a life of ease and without pain." But then Upāli's father and mother thought again: "If Upāli learns arithmetic, his breast will become diseased. But if Upāli could learn money-changing (*rūpa*), he would after our death live a life of ease and comfort and without pain." But then Upāli's father and mother said to themselves: "If Upāli learns money-changing, his eyes will suffer." The result was that it was decided that Upāli should

[1] J. G. Bühler, *Indian Palæography*, p. 6. [2] *Mahāvagga*, i. 49.

become a monk and join the *sangha*, and he and his companions were all admitted, but on account of their unruly conduct it was laid down that persons under twenty should not in future receive the full, or *upasampada*, ordination.

This passage seems to show that at the time when the *Mahāvagga* was composed it was not uncommon for some boys at least to learn writing and arithmetic, and that there were some facilities for this, and that these were outside the monasteries. It does not seem likely that at this time the monasteries had begun to be schools of popular instruction, and it is indeed probable that at first the only teaching given to those who joined the *sangha* was a knowledge of the precepts and doctrines of Buddhism. This passage bears witness to the existence of elementary schools of some sort, and it is remarkable that the three subjects of the curriculum mentioned bear a striking resemblance to those of the indigenous primary schools of India in much later times. *Lekhā* (writing),[1] *gaṇanā* (arithmetic, *i.e.* addition, subtraction, and the multiplication table) and *rūpa* (literally 'forms', but meaning arithmetic applied to simple commercial or agricultural purposes) are still the three subjects which are most prominent in the modern types of indigenous schools. According to the Elephant Cave inscription of the year 165 of the Mauryan era (about 157 or 148 B.C.), King Khāravela of Kalinga learnt these subjects in his childhood.[2] The *Lalita Vistara*[3] refers to the learning of writing and of the alphabet by children. *Jātaka*, No. 125, mentions the wooden writing-board (*phalaka*) known (as well as the *varṇaka*, or wooden pen) also to the *Lalita Vistara*, and still used in elementary schools.[4] There is a Sutta in Pāli which is called the *Sigalovāda Sutta*[5] which

[1] J. G. Bühler, *Indian Palæography*, p. 5. [2] *Ibid.*
[3] Ch. x. [4] Bühler, *op. cit.*, p. 5.
[5] Quoted in *Buddhism* (1890) by T. W. Rhys Davids. Translated in *Contemp. Rev.*, Feb., 1876, by Childers.

cnumerates the chief duties which men owe to one another in everyday life. Amongst the duties which are mentioned for parents are training their children in virtue and having them taught arts or sciences. It also contains a section which details the duties of pupils and teachers. The pupil should honour his teachers by rising in their presence, by ministering to them, by obeying them, by supplying their wants, by attention to instruction. The teacher should show his affection to his pupils, by training them in all that is good, by teaching them to hold knowledge fast, by instruction in science and lore, by speaking well of them to their friends and companions, by guarding them from danger. The mention among the duties of parents of having their children taught arts or science need imply no more than passing on to them the knowledge of their own particular craft or trade; but the mention of the duties of pupils and teachers in a manual relating to everyday life certainly seems to point to the existence of schools of some sort, though we cannot say that this implies the carrying on of secular instruction at the Buddhist monasteries. It seems rather to imply the existence of some facilities for popular instruction outside the monasteries, though not necessarily widespread.

The oldest known inscriptions in India are those of King Aśoka, who reigned from 272 to 231 B.C. This monarch had erected in various parts of India edicts and inscriptions on rocks and pillars, many of which have been discovered. His chief object was to promote amongst his people *Dharma* or moral duty. These inscriptions are in the vernacular. Aśoka also erected many monasteries. The existence of these edicts in the vernacular has been taken to imply that there was a widespread popular education going on in India at the time of Aśoka. Thus Mr. V. A. Smith says [1] that the care taken to publish the imperial edicts implies that a knowledge of reading

[1] *Aśoka*, p. 138.

and writing was widely diffused, and that there is the same inference from the inscriptions being in the vernacular. He says also that it is probable that learning was fostered by the numerous monasteries, and that boys and girls in hundreds of villages learned their lessons from the monks and nuns, as they do now in Burma, and that it is likely that the percentage of literacy among the Buddhist population in Aśoka's time was higher than it is now in many parts of British India. The vernacular inscriptions of Aśoka certainly seem to imply that there was a considerable amount of literacy, but what proportion of the population could read and write it seems quite impossible to conjecture. Even if only a few possessed these accomplishments it might have seemed quite worth while to Aśoka to erect his monuments and have inscriptions put on them, for the few could read them to the many. But it is very doubtful whether the Buddhist monasteries had become as early as this centres of a widespread popular instruction, and it is not certain that they ever became such in India. There is, however, evidence, as we have seen above, that before the time of Aśoka facilities of some kind existed for giving elementary instruction, and the welding together of a large part of India into one empire, under the strong rule of the Mauryan sovereigns, must have given increased opportunities for trade and commerce, and this may have also led to an increased demand for popular schools where the three R's could be learnt.

Buddhism placed both religion and education on a more popular basis than Brāhmanism, and by breaking down the monopoly of higher learning which had been in the hands of the Brāhman teachers, it may have also indirectly helped to increase the desire for primary education amongst the people. There was, moreover, about the first century of our era a most remarkable laymen's movement in India. This is illustrated by the production of the *Bhagavad Gītā*, which belongs to about that period, in which the possibility of the attainment of salvation by an earnest layman who does his duty is expounded, and also by the growth of the Mahāyāna form of Buddhism which holds out hopes of spiritual progress to those who are not able to forsake the world and become monks. This upheaval, both in Vaishṇavism and in Buddhism, is the evidence of a widespread movement amongst laymen in India, and it would be not unlikely that it would be also characterized by a growing desire for education. It is, perhaps, from this period that the Buddhist monasteries began to undertake secular as well as religious education, and there may also have been a large growth of popular elementary schools.

The effect of the Muhammadan domination upon these Hindu vernacular schools must have been considerable. The growth of a large Muhammadan population, who resorted to the Muhammadan *maktabs* for obtaining an elementary education, must have lessened their numbers, and the use of Persian as the official language by the Muhammadan rulers made even Hindus resort to Muhammadan teachers in order to obtain a knowledge of this language, and with it the possibility of obtaining Government employment. These Persian elementary schools must then have become numerous during the Muhammadan period, and the reference in the *Āīn-i-Akbarī* quoted above[1] shows that they were widespread at the time of Akbar. This extract does not refer to Hindu vernacular schools, although it mentions the Hindu Sanskrit education. But such schools, no doubt, continued, and would be used by the Hindu trading and agricultural classes. The school which Pietra della Valle saw[2] in South India in 1623, being held in a temple porch, was evidently a Hindu vernacular school. Adam in his report mentions[3] that one of the textbooks used in the Hindu vernacular schools was Subhankar's

[1] P. 124. [2] See p. 151.
[3] *Adam's Reports*, p. 97.

rhyming arithmetic rules, which he says was evidently composed during the existence of the Muhammadan power, as it was full of Persian terms and reference to Muhammadan usages. This shows how even the Hindu vernacular schools had to accommodate themselves to some extent to the altered circumstances which were brought about by the Muhammadan rule.

When the Education Commission of 1882 was conducting its investigations the witnesses were asked whether in their respective districts there existed an indigenous system of primary schools, and if so whether they were relics of an ancient village system. The replies given by witnesses in all provinces of India show great diversity of opinion. Some witnesses confidently affirmed that the primary schools were relics of an ancient village system, while others as confidently denied it. The evidence on which these opinions were based was not asked for, and very few of the witnesses attempted to support their opinions by any form of proof. The diversity of opinion can, however, be explained by the ambiguity of the question. The antiquity of this popular system, and its being a relic of an ancient village system, are really two distinct questions, and even the matter of antiquity largely depends on whether the system as a whole or separate schools are considered. The evidence seems to show that these schools were started in various places under various circumstances. There seems no reason to doubt, as we have already seen, that facilities for primary education existed in some places and among some classes even before the time of King Aśoka, but new schools were often springing up where they had not existed before, and sometimes a school might become defunct. The Muhammadan *maktabs* were in most cases closely connected with the mosque, but with regard to the Hindu vernacular schools it seems possible to trace at least four ways in which they came to be started.

(1) Some were connected with temples. The Bengal Report of the Education Commission of 1882 says[1]: 'Another class of educational institutions owed its origin to a different branch of the priesthood. Each village community of the Hindus had its tutelary idol with a Brāhman specially attached to its worship. Offering worship to the idol on behalf of all the different castes of the village people, this Brāhman naturally took under him in his tutorial capacity the children of all those who, as either belonging to or connected with the twice-born, felt themselves under the obligation to acquire letters. Thus originated the village *pāthśālas* which are still so much cherished by the people. The *pāthśāla* teacher subsisted on the *deottar* land of the idol, and received from his pupils free-will offerings and occasionally fees.' So in the Panjāb report also it is mentioned that some schools were connected with temples, and the school seen by Pietra della Valle was probably a temple school. That this, however, was not the only origin of such schools, even in the case of Bengal, is clear from Adam's reports. The schools were not always held in proximity to a temple, and both teachers and pupils included even the lowest castes.

(2) Other primary schools owed their origin to the enterprise of some village *zamīndār* or local magnate, who was anxious to have his own children taught, and was not unwilling to allow other children from the village to study under the same teacher along with his own children, and in some cases to allow the school to meet on the verandah of his house or in some other building that belonged to him.

(3) In other cases the school was started as a commercial venture by some enterprising person, who might be of any caste, in some place where he could secure sufficient pupils to make it worth his while to do so. This would be specially the case in the towns where trade and commerce would compel

[1] *Bengal Report*, p. 1.

many persons of all castes to desire a knowledge of the three R's.

(4) Sometimes, as in the case of the Mahājani schools,[1] a number of local traders would employ a teacher to teach their sons writing and accounts, so as to prepare them to follow their own calling. It is not unlikely that the earliest primary schools came into being in this way.

It does not then seem possible to speak of these indigenous primary schools, taken as a whole, as being the relic of an ancient village system. If they had been so we should expect to find that the teacher was in the same position as others in the village, like the carpenter, blacksmith, barber, village priest, and others, who receive fixed customary grants from the agricultural community of the village in return for the performances of their services, and pass on their rights from father to son. Not only did the manner of paying the teacher differ, generally at least, from the way that men of other professions and trades in the village received their remuneration, but the teachers were not confined to one caste, and there is little trace of their office being hereditary. In the case of a Brāhman teacher his position in the village community was no doubt due to his priestly office, and the ancient method of rewarding his services was continued even when he undertook vernacular teaching. But in the case of teachers of other castes, if in some cases they have established a similar position in a village community, it is hardly sufficient evidence in itself of the antiquity of the system. Apart from the Brāhmans there has never been a caste of teachers in India, and the teaching work of the Brāhmans was originally in connection with the Vedas and the higher Sanskrit learning given only to the three 'twice-born' castes rather than the imparting of primary education to all comers. It seems likely that the village primary school was an institution of

[1] For the Mahājani schools, see p. 73.

much later growth than other parts of the Indian village system.[1]

The character of these popular primary schools must have varied greatly in different places, and depended largely upon the efficiency and ability of the teacher. But as a whole they must have been very deficient, judged by modern European standards. They were intensely narrow in their outlook and had a strictly utilitarian aim. They had no idea of developing the higher mental life of their pupils or cultivating their æsthetic tastes. Any thought of helping the pupil to improve his character or realize the best that was in him was at most only a very secondary aim. The purpose was merely to enable the pupil to acquire sufficient mastery of reading, writing, and arithmetic, and a few applications of these, such as the composition of letters and business documents or the keeping of simple accounts, as would enable him to perform successfully the business of life. Subjects rather than pupils were taught. Memorizing of rules and tables was given a very prominent place. Even where, as in the Persian schools, some literature was included in the curriculum, there was no real cultivation of literary taste.

Moral and religious instruction was not apparently given very much place. The Muhammadan *maktabs* taught the Korān, but it seems to have been often little more than the memorizing of those passages necessary for the performance of Muhammadan devotions. The Hindu vernacular elementary schools were unconnected with the ancient system of Brāhmanic education. The Saraswatī Bandana, or salutation to the goddess of learning, was learnt by heart in some of these schools, and repeated by the whole school each day, and where the teacher was a temple priest, or other Brāhman, he may have given to his pupils incidentally a certain amount of

[1] For a different view, see *Village Government in British India*, by Mr. John Matthai, ch. ii.

instruction in the mythology and sacred lore of the Hindus, but beyond this there does not seem to have been much attention paid to the moral and religious side of education.

The discipline, as a rule, was not satisfactory, and the position of the teacher as dependent almost entirely on the fees or gifts he received from parents, or the good will of a *zamīndār* or other patron, was such that he was almost bound to become subservient and lacking in independence. Indian boys are often more passive than their Western cousins, but by no means without the desire of playing mischief when opportunity arises. In his Introduction to *Adam's Reports*, the Rev. J. Long quotes[1] from the *Calcutta Review* an account of some of the tricks played on teachers by Indian boys. Among them are the following. In preparing the teacher's hookah boys mix the tobacco with chillies and other pungent ingredients, so that when he smokes he is made to cough violently, while the whole school is convulsed with laughter. Or beneath the mat on which he sits may be strewn thorns and sharp prickles, which soon display their effect in the contortions of the crest-fallen and discomfited master. Some of the forms of punishment mentioned in the same number of the *Calcutta Review* as formerly common in Indian schools strike one as particularly brutal. The following are examples. A boy was made to bend forward with his face to the ground; a heavy stick was then placed on his back and another on his neck; and should he let either of them fall, within the prescribed period of half an hour or so, he was punished with the cane. A boy was made to hang for a few minutes with his head downwards from the branch of a neighbouring tree. A boy was put in a sack along with some nettles, or a cat, or some other noisome creature, and then rolled along the ground. A boy was made to measure so many cubits on the ground, by marking it along with the tip of his nose. It must be hoped

[1] Introd. to *Adam's Reports*, pp. 10 ff.

that such punishments were used only on rare occasions with the most recalcitrant offenders, or that the very possibility of their being inflicted was sufficient to preserve discipline.

In spite, however, of many deficiencies and weaknesses, there were many good points about these schools which must not be overlooked. Individual rather than class teaching was the rule, and each pupil was free to develop at his own speed according to his own intellectual power. In small schools, such as they were, with pupils of varying age, this must have been a distinct advantage. The employment of monitors to help the master must have been a most valuable means not only of helping him in his work, but of giving the more promising pupils a training in responsibility and also an opportunity for testing and practising the skill they themselves had acquired. The teachers, if somewhat narrow in their intellectual capacity, and dependent upon the good will of those who employed them, seem to have been nevertheless hardworking and conscientious, and although their aim was not very wide, it seems to have been accomplished. The schools were closely connected with life outside the school, and teaching for the most part only that 'useful knowledge' which is so highly regarded by the 'man in the street,' they had no temptation to develop theories of formal discipline. If some of the methods employed in teaching were antiquated and unsatisfactory judged by modern standards, others were fully in accordance with modern theory. In the Montessori system we find it advocated that writing should be taught before reading, and that in teaching to write the child should first be made constantly to run his fingers over grooved or sandpaper letters in order to fix the forms in the muscular memory. Both these ideas were long ago current in Indian schools. We have already had occasion to refer to this in connection with the extract from the *Āīn-i-Akbarī*[1]; and in

[1] See p. 125.

the description of some of those primary schools in the early part of this chapter it has been shown how a boy is taught to learn his letters by writing them with a small stick on sand, and not by pronouncing them, and how he learns to write by tracing over the letters already made by the master with an iron style. It must be remembered also that these schools, though they might receive help from a local patron, had no public grants for their support. With only the shade of a tree, or a verandah, for schoolroom, with hardly any manuscripts, and practically no school apparatus except a few plantain or palm leaves or a little paper and a few styles for writing, with a mere pittance for their support, and with a meagre intellectual training, it must be admitted that the results achieved by the teachers of these primary schools were not altogether unworthy, and they helped through long centuries to give to India some elements of a popular education, and to prepare for that time when it should be possible for education to become more widespread among the people.

Although the Hindu primary vernacular schools were unconnected with the Brāhmanic schools of higher learning, they probably derived many of their ideas of teaching as well as their methods from those schools; but as the Brāhmanic learning tended more and more to be separated from the ordinary concerns of life, they supplied a popular want which would not otherwise have been met. And if they did not concern themselves very much with the teaching of religion, it must be remembered that there has always been in India a wide diffusion of moral truths and religious ideas by means of the allegories and fables (like those of the *Panchatantra* and the *Hitopadeśa*), and the epic poems (*Rāmāyaṇa*, etc.), which are handed down from generation to generation by means of the family and the social intercourse of the people as they gather in the evening, after the day's work is done, for gossip and song and story.

The introduction of education on modern lines has had a far-reaching effect on this popular indigenous system of elementary education. Different policies were adopted in different provinces with regard to it. In some provinces these schools were slowly replaced by new schools instituted by Government, or at least under Government inspection. In other provinces they were reformed and absorbed into the modern system. One still hears, even nowadays, of a school being started, as a pecuniary venture by an enterprising teacher, or by a *zamīndār* or other local magnate for his own children and others; but such schools can seldom survive for long without the aid of a Government grant, which means that they become absorbed in the general Government system of education. Still, even in the schools most closely under Government inspection and control, many of the features of the old indigenous schools, both good and bad, can still be traced.

CHAPTER VI

SOME GENERAL CONCLUSIONS

In the previous chapters some account has been given of the various systems of education which have been in vogue in India in bygone ages. Many traces and relics of these ancient systems are still indeed to be found in India, and some parts of them at least are still in full working order. But the progress and spread of education on Western lines has curtailed their activity to a very large extent, and tends more and more to limit the spheres within which they are operative. Few countries, and certainly no Western ones, have had systems of education which have had such a long and continuous history with so few modifications as some of the educational systems of India. The long centuries through which they have held sway show that they must have possessed elements which were of value, and that they were not unsuited to the needs of those who developed and adopted them. They produced many great men and earnest seekers after truth, and their output on the intellectual side is by no means inconsiderable. They developed many noble educational ideals, which are a valuable contribution to educational thought and practice. But the early vigour, which showed itself in the great contributions which India made to the science of grammar and mathematics, and philosophy and other subjects, had long since spent itself when that momentous change began, which was brought about by the introduction of Western education and learning. The Brāhmanic educational system had become stereotyped and formal and unable to meet the needs of a progressive civilization. We have then to seek for the causes of its decay and failure and the reasons why it was unsuitable for present-day conditions in India. But we must also seek to understand what elements of permanent value it possessed and what contributions it has to make to the educational thought of the world in general and India in particular. In considering these questions we shall be most concerned with the Brāhmanic system and the education of special classes of the Hindu community which were more or less connected with it, as this is the oldest system, and also that which has had most effect upon India as a whole. Buddhist education was an offshoot from the Brāhmanic education, and very closely connected with it in ideals and practice; while the Muhammadan education was a foreign system which was transplanted to India, and grew up in its new soil with very little connection with, or influence upon, the Brāhmanic system, and was, with a few exceptions, open only to that minority of the population which embraced the Muhammadan faith.

If education is described as a preparation for life, or for complete living, we may say that the ancient Indian educators would fully have accepted this doctrine. But it would have included preparation not only for this life, but also for a future existence. The harmonizing of these two purposes in due proportions has always been a difficult task for educators. If it could be perfectly accomplished many of the problems of education would be solved. But in practice there has always been oscillation. Thus in the Middle Ages in Europe stress was laid upon preparation for the world to come, while modern European systems often tend unduly to ignore this side of education. India has had the same problem to face, and has had similar difficulties in meeting it. The young Brāhman was being prepared by the education he received for his practical duties in life as a priest and teacher of others, but the need of preparing himself for the life after death was also included in the teaching he received. The same may be said of the young Kshatriyas and Vaiśyas who were required not only to fit themselves for their practical work in life, but also to study the Vedas, and give heed to the teaching of religion.

Owing, however, to the current philosophy which taught the unreality of this world of time, and that the highest wisdom was to seek release from the worldly fetters which held the soul in bondage, and that the highest knowledge was to become acquainted with the method by which release could be obtained, there was a tendency to despise the practical duties of life and the preparation for them. The idea of the four stages, or *āśramas*, seems to have been formulated to try and check this tendency by inculcating the desirability of a student passing to the state of a householder before he became a forest hermit or wandering ascetic ; but many passed straight from the student life to the life of complete renunciation of the world, and the *Upanishads* show us how there was a tendency amongst the more earnest to despise the ordinary learning of the schools and preparation for this life in comparison with the higher philosophic knowledge which was concerned with the life beyond. This was not confined to the Brāhmans, but Kshatriyas and others also were affected by this movement, and the two religions of Jainism and Buddhism were founded by Kshatriyas. Buddhism also, in encouraging the life of meditation and the joining of an order of monks, was, like Brāhmanic philosophy, setting forth an ideal of life which despised, or regarded as unreal, this fleeting world of time, and hence made that education which was a preparation for the practical duties of life, something on a lower plane than that which was a preparation for the other world.

The underlying conception of all this philosophic thought

which had such a profound influence upon Indian education was the doctrine of transmigration of souls and of *karma*. According to this doctrine the result of all actions, good or bad, has to be reaped in this life or in a life to come, and our present life is governed by our actions in a previous life. So long as there are actions the fruits of which have to be reaped, a man is condemned to be born and reborn in different forms of life, ascending or descending in the scale, and this weary round of existence goes on unceasingly unless a man can in some way obtain release and cut the chain of transmigration. This doctrine, in slightly different forms, is held by all the recognized philosophical schools of Hinduism, as well as by Buddhism and Jainism, and the main purpose of their philosophy was to discover the true way by which deliverance might be accomplished. In some phases of Indian philosophy the World is regarded as an illusion, or *Māyā*, and the only real existence is an impersonal Unknown, or Brahman. We are not here concerned with the truth or otherwise of these philosophic conceptions, nor with the various ways which were set forth for the obtaining of salvation, but it must be observed that their influence upon the intellectual life of India was such as to turn intellectual effort almost entirely in one direction, and other studies were regarded as chiefly of value in preparation for, and as leading up to, these higher truths. There was thus a cramping of thought, and although there were not wanting those who gave their attention to other branches of learning, many of the most earnest and brilliant of Indian scholars spent their life in speculating upon these philosophic conceptions. The spirit of other-worldliness which thus gained a hold upon the Brāhmanic schools made them more and more out of touch with the ordinary life of the world, and helped to make them unfit to mould the Indian peoples in the paths of progress and general culture

It is obvious, however, that if all were to forsake the world for a hermit or monastic life the bonds of society would soon be broken, and the work of the world come to a stop. It was to meet this difficulty, as we have seen, that it was prescribed that the general practice should be for a student to become a householder before entering upon the ascetic life; but there was also another doctrine formulated, which gave comfort to those who felt themselves unable to forsake the world, by admitting that if a man performed well the duties of the station in which he was born he might progress spiritually on condition that he kept himself from attachment to the things of the world. Thus in the *Bhagavad Gītā*, when the young Kshatriya warrior Arjuna is about to go into battle and feels some qualms with regard to engaging in a strife against relatives, Kṛishna, who has appeared to him in the form of a charioteer, encourages him to do his duty. He urges upon him the doctrine that in performing all social and religious duties of his caste in a spirit of indifference, and without the least regard for the direct or indirect results which may accrue from them, he may be freed from the necessity of reaping the fruit which would otherwise attach to them, and progress towards union with the Supreme.

'In works be thine office; in their fruits must it never be. Be not moved by the fruits of works; but let not attachment to worklessness dwell in thee.' [1]

'The man who casts off all desires and walks without desire, with no thought of a Mine or of an I, comes into peace.' [2]

Whatever may have been the truth or falsehood of the underlying philosophy of this doctrine, it was not one that would tend towards intellectual or educational progress.

The very idea, moreover, of each man being born to perform certain functions in life according to his caste tended

[1] *Bhagavad Gītā*, ii. 47 (Dr. Barnett's trans.). [2] *Ibid.*, ii. 71.

to a narrowing of the purpose of education, and to its being regarded as chiefly concerned with preparing a boy to fulfil the duties of his particular occupation in life. Thus while, on the one hand, the underlying philosophic thought tended towards a spirit of other-worldliness and to education being conceived as a preparation for what lay beyond this life, on the other hand it tended towards a narrow vocationalism, and those especially who were shut out from the study of the Vedas and the higher philosophical thought received little direct religious education, and their training was confined to the acquisition of those subjects or mechanical arts which they needed for their caste occupation. Thus for the mass of the people education came to be regarded from a narrowly utilitarian point of view, and when the popular elementary schools grew up to provide for the need of simple instruction for the commercial and agricultural classes, they also, like the caste training, were largely utilitarian in their outlook. Even the Brāhmanic schools often tended to become utilitarian, and those who attended them were often aiming at gaining just that knowledge which would enable them to earn their livelihood, either in connection with the performance of religious rites for the people, or in the service of the State. It is not, of course, to be understood that there was no religious basis for the education of those who were not aiming at the life of absolute renunciation of the world. Far from it. The deeply religious nature of the Indian peoples has led them to surround all actions of life with religious associations, and even those who were shut out from the study of the Vedas had their religious rites. These indeed often were connected with the grossest idolatry and superstition, which became, however, parts of the Hindu system, and the very fact that the highest ideals were possible only for the few gave these lower forms of religion a greater opportunity to spread amongst the people.

The doctrine of transmigration and *karma* on the one hand may have tended to set before men a high moral standard by making them feel the importance of all actions, as the fruit of these had to be reaped at some time or other; but in its more extreme form the doctrine taught that even good actions, as well as bad, were to be avoided, for the fruit of these also would have to be reaped, and so the cycle of births would have to be prolonged. Thus India came under the sway of a philosophy of pessimism which allowed little place in the universe for the action of Providence, or the working of moral purpose, and there was little to encourage men to progress or hopeful endeavour. In the early Vedic times life was more joyous and free, and this was the time when great intellectual movements began in India. But as the gloomy view of existence came to have more and more hold over Indian life and thought the sap of intellectual effort dried up and the progress of civilization was arrested. Hence the early promise of the ancient Brāhmanic education, with its many noble ideals and possibilities of development, was not fulfilled, and it was led into a more and more narrow groove, and was incapable of supplying the needs of a progressive and advancing civilization.

The philosophic conceptions of the doctrine of transmigration also underlay the caste system, which was justified and explained on the ground that a man was born into a particular caste according to his merits or demerits in a previous existence. The caste system indeed was not without its good points. It gave stability to society, and established guilds which preserved learning and craftsmanship. It was a system of mutual responsibility, and the richer members of the caste were expected to stand behind the poorer members in case of need. But, on the other hand, it discouraged originality and enterprise, and promoted stagnation and division. There was no possibility for a man to pass from one caste to another, and hence on its educational side it was the narrowest form of vocational training the world has ever seen. There was no incentive for a boy to rise above a certain level, and no freedom of intercourse amongst the different occupations. In this narrow vocational system there was no idea of general culture or of study for the sake of study, nor was there the possibility of new avenues of learning being opened up. The individual was being educated not so much for his own sake as for the sake of society, and individualism had very little scope, if any, for development.

Brāhmanic education, as well as other forms of education in India, looked to the past for its ideals rather than to the future. Whatever variations or new ideas were permitted within Brāhmanism, it was always on the two conditions that the absolute authority of the Vedas should be recognized, and also the supremacy of the Brāhman priesthood. And so in education also it was the ideals of the past which ever governed its development. The duty of the teacher was to pass on as nearly as he himself had received it the mass of tradition which had been handed down from past ages. As this increased in bulk, and specialization became necessary, it was still the past to which the student was taught to look for guidance, and the ancient standards were regarded as authoritative. Thus in grammar, after the great work of Pāṇini and Patanjali the science became fixed, and though an enormous number of works on grammar have been written in India since, it was always recognized that these ancient authorities must not be departed from. Education also became stereotyped, and the same methods which were followed hundreds of years before the Christian era continued with little change down to modern times.

In criticizing the ancient Indian education one can say that it had many of the same defects that the education of

Europe had before the Revival of Learning, and like that education it needed some new breath of life to quicken it and transform it. In the case of India that new force has come from the West in the introduction of Western learning and Western ideas. India is at present passing through a period of intellectual, social, political, and religious ferment which is in many ways similar to the change through which Europe passed during the Renaissance. In no direction has the change been more apparent than in education. Schools on Western lines started by Government, or missionary societies, or Muhammadan or Hindu associations, or other bodies, have not only spread all over India, but have been welcomed and highly appreciated by the people, and there is an increasing demand for even greater facilities. The education of girls has indeed been slow in its progress compared with that which has been made in the education of boys, and the technical training of the craftsmen still proceeds very much on the old lines. Moreover, the Brāhmanic learning is still being passed on to a few in the old traditional way, and the Muhammadan *maktabs* still give instruction to the young Muhammadans in the Korān. But more and more the Western education advances, and there is a danger lest educational practices and ideals which have been found useful in Europe should be regarded as being of necessity equally suited to the needs of India. This is not always the case, and it may be that as education progresses in India many of the ideals which were worked out by ancient Indian educators will reassert themselves, and in a modern form, and in conjunction with many Western ideals may prove of great service to those engaged in the great task of educating the rising generation of India.

One of the most characteristic of Indian educational ideals is the relation between pupil and teacher. This relationship receives a great deal of attention in the ancient books, both Hindu and Buddhist. Great reverence and respect is required from the pupil, while the teacher on his part has also high responsibilities. The idea of this relationship of pupil to teacher has indeed been sometimes so developed that it has led to the teacher, or *guru*, receiving divine honours from his pupil, or disciple, in some forms of Hinduism, and sects which have sprung from it. In a more sober conception of this relationship, it is thought of as that of father and son, and so far was this idea carried out that the pupil was considered to be in a closer relation to the teacher than to his real father. The pupil often resided at the house of his teacher, and, even when this was not the case, was always in close contact with him. The paternal relationship of the teacher towards the pupil was emphasized by the absence of any regular fee. The teacher, having accepted the responsibility of the position, was considered morally bound to perform his duty towards the pupil, and moreover in the case of the Brāhman preceptor, to teach was a duty which he owed to society. The pupil, on the other hand was carrying out the filial relationship not only in the respect he paid to the teacher, but also in attending to the service of his household. The ideal is thus a domestic one, and it is quite foreign to the Indian system that there should be a large institution or a large class of pupils taught together. The Indian ideal would seem to be one teacher for each pupil, and though on practical grounds this may not often have been realized, yet so far as the evidence is available, we find, as a rule, quite a small number of pupils taught by each teacher. Where there was a centre of learning corresponding to a university, this seems to have been a collection of such small classes grouped in one place. The same teacher, moreover, generally taught the pupil from the beginning to the end of the period of learning. In the West it is the institution rather than the teacher which is emphasized, and it is the school or college which a student regards as his *alma mater.* In India it is the teacher rather than the institution that is prominent, and the same affection and reverence which a Western student has for his *alma mater* is in India bestowed with a life-long devotion upon the teacher. Even the introduction of Western education with its many teachers, and many classes, has not entirely broken down this ideal, in spite of the complications which it produces. To an Indian student a teacher who only appears at stated hours to teach or lecture, and is not accessible at all times to answer questions and give advice on all manner of subjects, is an anomaly. Such a relationship, no doubt, throws a greatly increased responsibility upon the teacher, and where the teacher is not worthy of his position may be attended with grave dangers. But where the teacher is a man who reaches a high intellectual, moral, and spiritual standard. there is much to be said for the Indian ideal. There is no country in the world where the responsibilities and opportunities of the teacher are greater than they are in India.

Closely connected with the family relationship which exists between teacher and pupil is the employment of monitors to assist the teacher in his instruction. These fulfil the place of elder brothers of the family. The monitorial system of Bell and Lancaster, which Bell is said to have devised by seeing the method used in schools in India, is but a caricature of the Indian ideal. In English schools the prefectual system has associated the elder boys with the masters in the government and discipline of the school, and it is generally recognized as being one of the most valuable parts of their training. According to the Indian idea the more advanced scholars are associated with the master in the work of teaching, and though the system may have been originally devised to help the master in solving the problem of teaching several pupils at different stages at the same time, it must have been a valuable training for the monitors themselves. In India the bullying of younger boys by older ones is almost unknown, and the respect shown by the younger boys towards the older boys is very marked. The resuscitation of this ancient Indian ideal of monitors would therefore be worth a trial, and it is not unlikely that it might show very excellent results if the conditions were also fulfilled that the class should be small, and that it was composed of pupils all at different stages of progress.

An ideal of Indian life which has a close bearing on education is that which has been happily termed *naissance oblige.*[1] The evils of the caste system are indeed manifest, and have already been referred to; but we must not overlook the fact that it has also had its useful side, and from the educational point of view it has brought about a vast system of vocational training which was made possible by the fact that a boy's future career was determined from his very birth, for upon his birth depended both his duties and privileges in life. Moreover, this vocational training was permeated by the idea of the family, and was carried out under conditions which brought it into close contact with life. The decay of the caste system, with all its attendant evils, seems inevitable under the conditions of modern life. But it is to be hoped that as it passes some of its nobler phases may be preserved, and that the vocational idea of education which it has fostered may not be lost. The tendency to extend a uniform system and so to reduce all education to the dead level of a code-bound type is already at work in India, and the ideal of vocational training needs to be made much more prominent. How to develop a system of vocational education which may incorporate the best elements of the old ideals with the claims of modern education is no easy problem, but it is one which will have eventually to be faced.

Those who study India from the point of view of its

[1] See Farquhar, *Crown of Hinduism*, p. 203.

philosophy alone may get the impression that the people of India are a race of impractical dreamers who spend much of their time in meditating on lofty abstractions. That philosophical speculation has been carried to a very high point in India is of course true, but the practical side of life has also been cultivated, and a great deal of social life has been permeated by utilitarianism. In education this is reflected in the vocational ideals to which we have referred. But the spiritual basis which underlies life is never left out of sight, and in the ultimate analysis is regarded as paramount. The great difficulty which the people of India have felt has been to preserve a unity between the spiritual and the practical point of view, and this has often led to impractical otherworldliness on the one hand and narrow vocationalism on the other. But no view of life would be regarded as adequate which did not rest ultimately on a spiritual basis, and hence in education it is regarded as essential that a pupil's life should be lived in a religious environment and permeated by religious ideals. It is this which creates a very difficult problem for a Government which seeks to preserve a strictly neutral attitude in religious matters.

The Brāhmanic settlements were probably most frequently situated in forests in ancient times. The contact with nature and absence of the evils of city life which this involved must have been important factors in creating an atmosphere which was most helpful in the formation of spiritual ideals. The classic poets love to depict the beautiful surroundings of the *āśramas* and the simple life of their innabitants in contact with both animate and inanimate nature. Though the Brāhmanic education was no doubt also carried on in towns, especially in later times, the forest sanctuary has always been the Indian ideal. This is another of the ancient educational ideals which is most important, and one that is worthy of the attention of modern educationists.

The main purpose of this book has been to trace the development of the ancient Indian systems of education, and in emphasizing some of the ideals which they have worked out no attempt is made to be exhaustive, nor to show all the bearings which the ancient ideals have on present conditions. This would need a book to itself. There can be no doubt, however, that the development of India's future educational ideals will not be governed solely by Western educational thought and practice, and in education as in all other phases of social life a mingling of East and West is not only inevitable but desirable.[1] Experience alone will determine how this can be done with the least possible friction and waste of effort. It may not, however, be out of place to indicate what seems to the author of this book the plane upon which European and Asian thought may best be brought together in education as well as in other matters. This is best shown by the following quotation :—

'Christianity is the religion which associates East and West in a higher range of thought than either can reach alone, and tends to substitute a peaceful union for the war into which the essential difference of Asiatic and European character too often leads the two continents. So profound is the difference, that in their meeting either war must result, or each of them must modify itself. There is no power except religion strong enough to modify both sufficiently to make a peaceful union possible ; and there is no religion but Christianity which is wholly penetrated both with the European and with the Asiatic spirit—so penetrated that many are sensitive only to one or the other. . . . It is now becoming plain to all that the relation of Asia to Europe is in process

[1] Two interesting educational experiments, which are attempts to combine some of the ancient educational ideals of India with those which have been received from the West, are the *Ārya Samāj Gurukula* at Hardwar, and Sir Rabindranath Tagore's *Shāntiniketan* at Bolpur.

of being profoundly changed; and very soon this will be a matter of general discussion. The long-unquestioned domination of European over Asiatic is now being put to the test, and is probably coming to an end. What is to be the issue? That depends entirely on the influence of Christianity, and on the degree to which it has affected the aims both of Christian and of non-Christian nations; there are cases in which it has affected the latter almost more than the former. The ignorant European fancies that progress for the East lies in Europeanizing it. The ordinary traveller in the East can tell that it is as impossible to Europeanize the Asiatic as it is to make an Asiatic out of an European, but he has not learned that there is a higher plane on which Asia and Europe may "mix and meet". . . . The new stage towards which Christianity is moving, and in which it will be better understood than it has been by purely European thought, will be a synthesis of European and Asiatic nature and ideas.' [1]

The future of India lies in its children, and this land, with its vast population, presents a wonderful opportunity as well as a huge responsibility to its educators. There are, and will no doubt always be, many controversies with regard to the most desirable development that its educational system shall take; but it is to be hoped that there will arise therefrom a system which, while incorporating new and old, will transcend both in its practice as well as in its ideals.

[1] *The Letters to the Seven Churches of Asia*, Sir W. M. Ramsay, 1904, Preface, pp. v. ff.

BIBLIOGRAPHY

A LARGE number of books on Indian history, literature, and religions contain occasional references to the ancient systems of education, and also supply the necessary background. Some of these are mentioned in the footnotes. The following books contain some of the more important references.

For General Outlines of the Ancient Systems.

Graves, F. P. *A History of Education* (vol. i.).
Laurie, S. S. *Historical Survey of Pre-Christian Education.*
Monroe, P. *Cyclopædia of Education.*
Hastings' *Encyclopædia of Religion and Ethics.*

For Brāhmanic Education.

Hastings' *Encyclopædia of Religion and Ethics* (article on '*Āśrama*').
Volumes in the Sacred Books of the East (edited by F. Max Müller).
Vols. i. and xv. *The Upanishads* (translated by F. Max Müller).
Vol. ii. *The Sūtras of Āpastamba and Gautama* (translated by J. G. Bühler).
Vol. xiv. *The Dharmasūtras of Vasishṭha and Baudhāyana* (translated by J. G. Bühler).
Vols. xii., etc. *The Śatapatha Brāhmaṇa* (translated by Eggeling).
Vol. xxv. *The Law Code of Manu* (translated by J. G. Bühler).
Müller, F. Max. *Lectures on the Origin of Religion.*
,, ,, *Sanskrit Literature.*
Macdonell, A. A. *Sanskrit Literature.*
Adam, William. *Reports on Vernacular Education in Bengal*, 1835–1838 (edited by Rev. J. Long, 1868).
Ward, William. *A View of the Hindoos.*
Nadiā Gazetteer (*Bengal District Gazetteers*, No. 24), 1916.

For Education of Special Classes of the Community.

Kauṭilya's *Arthaśāstra.* Translated by R. Shamasastry.
Coomaraswamy, A. K. *The Indian Craftsman.*
Birdwood, Sir Geo. C. M. *The Industrial Arts of India.*
The Dharmasūtras (as above).
The Law Code of Manu (as above).

For Buddhist Education.

Beal, A. *Buddhist Recoras of the Western World* (translation of the *Travels of Hiuen Tsiang*).

Legge, J. *Fāhien* (*A Record of Buddhistic Kingdoms*).

Takakusu, I. *A Record of the Buddhist Religion* (*Travels of I. Tsing*).

Childers, F. Article in *Contemp. Rev.*, Feb., 1876, with translation of *Sigalowāda Sutta.*

Sacred Books of the East, vols. xiii., xvii., xx., *Vinaya Texts* (translated by Rhys Davids, and Oldenberg).

Satish Chandra Vidyabhusana. *History of the Mediæval School of Indian Logic.*

For Muhammadan Education.

Narendra Nath Law. *Promotion of Learning in India during Muhammadan Rule.*

Āīn-i-Akbarī. Translated by H. Blochmann.

Bernier, F. *Travels in the Mogul Empire* (translated by A. Constable).

Adam, W., *Reports* (as above).

For Primary Education.

Adam, W. *Reports* (as above).

Gover, C. E. Article in *Indian Antiquary*, Feb., 1873 (ii. 52) on 'Pyal Schools in Madras'.

Report of Education Commission of 1882 (with appendices relating to different provinces).

Quinquennial Review of Education in India, 1907–1912.

Satthianadhan, S. *History of Education in the Madras Presidency.*

Thomas, F. W. *The History and Prospects of British Education in India.*

Matthai, J. *Village Government in British India* (ch. ii.).

Bühler, J. G. *Indian Palæography.*

INDEX